Survey of Corporate Contributions, 1990 Edition

by Maureen Nevin Duffy

A Research Report from The Conference Board

Contents

Method Tables

Canadian Tables

From the President

Major corporations responding to this *Survey of Corporate Contributions* reported contributions totaling over $1.6 billion. Expectations are that 1989 contributions will increase from the previous year. The Conference Board's *Survey of Corporate Contributions*, now in its twenty-third edition, provides executives with a detailed, comprehensive overview of corporate contributions based on information provided by 356 firms. As a budgeting and planning tool, this report enables executives to assess their programs against those of other firms in their industry, firms with the same income or asset size, or firms in their region of the country, and also to evaluate national trends.

This report includes charts that present important highlights graphically and succinctly. Trends in noncash contributions, corporate assistance, foundation grants, and corporate priorities, for example, are easier to follow through such charts.

The Conference Board appreciates the participation of the contributions executives who supply data for this survey every year. Their sustained support is essential to the quality of the information we are able to report.

PRESTON TOWNLEY
President

Highlights

Contributions as a median percent of:

	('88)	('87)
U.S. pretax income	0.9	1.05
Worldwide pretax income	0.8	0.9

Where they gave:

Share of Contributions Dollars Received	('88)	('87)
Education	37.3%	36.8%
Health & Human Services	29.2	27.2
Civic & Community	12.9	14.2
Culture & Art	11.2	10.8
Other	7.2	11
Unspecified	2.2	n/a

The Givers—U.S. Industries (356 Firms)

Ranked By Size of Contribution

Industrial Machinery and Computer (16)	$203,979,000
Petroleum & Gas (20)	178,522,000
Transportation Equipment (19)	158,933,000
Pharmaceuticals (17)	149,695,000
Retail/Wholesale (15)	147,529,000
Telecommunications (12)	119,604,000
Banking (43)	112,972,000
Other Manufacturing (30)	99,938,000
Chemicals (16)	89,465,000
Insurance (39)	80,882,000
Food, Beverage & Tobacco (12)	58,830,000
Paper Products (15)	53,524,000
Utilities (47)	44,096,000
Finance (6)	38,231,000
Printing and Publishing (6)	36,892,000
Business Services (18)	32,426,000
Electrical Machinery, except Computers (10)	22,150,000
Transportation (7)	14,311,000
Textiles (4)	3,711,000

How Much They Gave

Programs in 1988 ranged in size from $35,000 to $75 million, with a median contributions budget of about $1,210,000. The sum total of giving by all responding companies was $1.646 billion.

What they gave—Cash 89%, Securities 1%, Product 7%, Property and Equipment, 3%.

Total number of U.S. respondents 356

Contributions per Employee

A median drawn from the responses of 279 participants showed that gifts per employee are up—$173 per employee from $157 in 1987. (Note that reduced staff will boost the amount per employee if the budget stays the same.)

The per employee median for companies with under 1,000 employees fell more than 50%, from $425 in 1987 to $202 in 1988. This figure should be viewed with caution since the sample changed and the number of respondents in this group was small.

Administrative Costs

The median cost of running the contributions function went from $99,900 in 1987 to $83,500 in 1988. There has been a 40% drop since 1986. As a percentage of the charitable contributions budget, median administrative costs in 1988 ranged from 5%—10% of contributions (see Table 12). Budgets from $500,000 to $1 million reported the highest percentage of administrative cost.

Overseas Giving

In 1988, 113 companies reported contributions outside the U.S. Eighty-five companies (24% of respondents) reported dollars spent. The median donation of $174,000 was up slightly. Individual company contributions ranged from $400,000 to nearly $45 million.

Restructuring

• Forty-two percent of firms represented in the survey report a major restructuring in the past five years.
• Of these, 60% said their budgets were not affected.
• For those whose budgets were affected, figures reported ranged from a reduction in budget of 60% to an increase of 300%, with the median being a drop of 21%.

Tax reform

• Two-thirds of respondents say the Tax Reform Act of 1986 had no effect on their current giving programs.

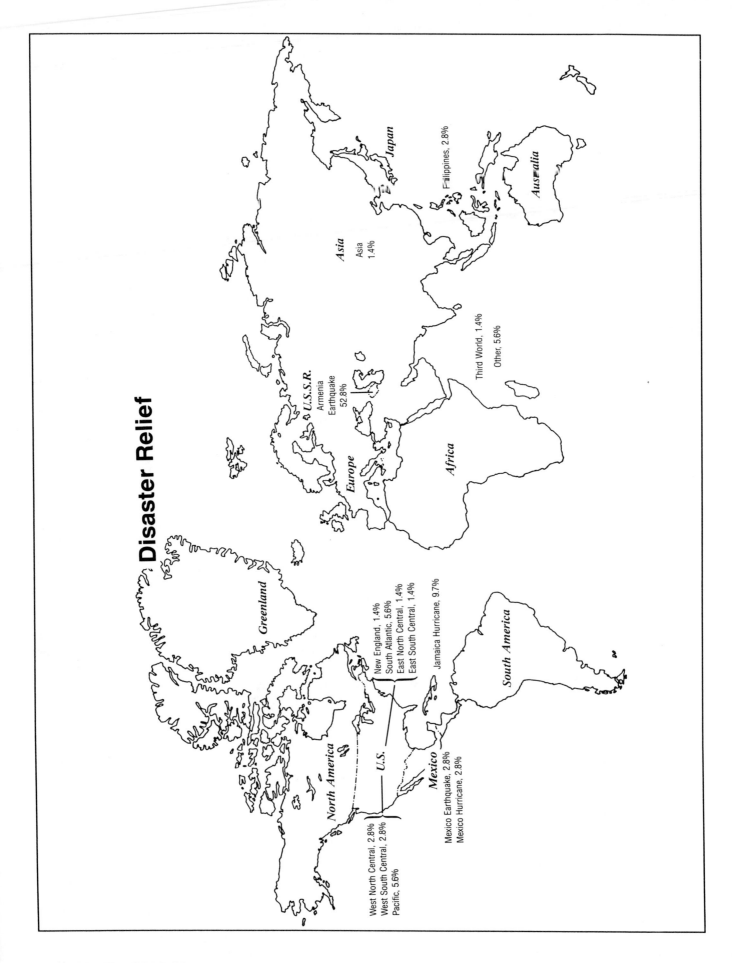

Disaster Relief

Greenland

North America

U.S.

Mexico

South America

U.S.S.R.

Europe

Africa

Asia

Japan

Australia

Armenia
Earthquake
52.8%

Asia
1.4%

Philippines, 2.8%

Third World, 1.4%
Other, 5.6%

New England, 1.4%
South Atlantic, 5.6%
East North Central, 1.4%
East South Central, 1.4%

Jamaica Hurricane, 9.7%

Mexico Earthquake, 2.8%
Mexico Hurricane, 2.8%

West North Central, 2.8%
West South Central, 2.8%
Pacific, 5.6%

Disaster relief

- $5,022,867 for disaster relief in 1988
- 53% to help Armenian earthquake victims. Jamaican hurricane relief received the next largest amount. (See map.)
- Pharmaceuticals reported the most in emergency relief: $3,215,000.

The Outlook for Corporate Contributions

Seventy-four percent of the companies reporting their anticipated budgets for 1989 thought they would be the same or greater than in 1988. Of those anticipating budgets the same or larger, the median increase is over 9 percent.

However, 39 of the 75 top donors in 1988 (companies with budgets of more than $5 million) expected to reduce contributions in 1989, with decreases ranging from less than 1% to nearly 60 percent.

Canadian Survey of Corporate Contributions

This year, for the first time in the 45-year history of this survey, The Conference Board, Inc. collaborated with The Conference Board of Canada to measure corporate charitable donations by Canada-based corporations.

A total of 111 companies out of a mailing of 522 responded (just over 20 percent). Participants were split nearly evenly among:

- manufacturing (59)
- and nonmanufacturing (52)
- 86% are in the top 500 of *Canadian Business*

Total Contributions: $75 million
Median Contributions: $275 thousand

- Cash—$64 million
- Product—$4 million
- Property and Equipment—$450 thousand
- Foundation Grants—$4.7 million

Canadian companies gave most heavily to Health & Human Services and Education. (See table on page 59.)
Corporate Assistance—$5 million, median $50,000

Canadian Crisis Relief

Canadian corporations also reported gifts intended to alleviate the effects of natural disasters—in Armenia, Ethiopia, Jamaica and Edmonton, Alberta, which was hit by tornadoes. Twelve of the 111 Canadian survey respondents gave for disaster relief. Nine Canadian respondents reported combined donations of $158,732 to disasters in 1988.

Contributions Outside Canada

- $6,081,811 by 23 corporations, median donation $48,012

Anticipated Giving by Canada-based Corporations in 1989

To All—up 6.44% (104 companies)
To Education—up 3.41% (91 companies)

Survey Administration

The questionnaire used to collect 1988 data was essentially the same as the 1987 form in order to retain year-to-year comparability of information, with the addition of some specific questions on disaster relief, tax reform, and corporate restructuring. Data on corporate income, sales, and assets come from participants or annual reports and other public sources.

Questionnaires were sent to the 1989 Fortune 500 manufacturing and the Fortune 500 service companies, as well as other large corporations from in-house lists. The sample also included corporations that have participated in past surveys.

The questionnaire was mailed in March of 1989 and addressed to a named contributions manager whenever possible. If no name was available, a cover letter was sent to "Corporate Contributions Executive." Non-respondents were sent a second mailing in May.

Surveys were also mailed to 522 Canada-based corporations and 112 corporations responded with usable data. (See results on pages 53-63.)

A total of 356 usable questionnaires were returned with 1988 data—a response rate of 14%. Twenty-eight more companies responded this year than in 1987. The aggregate contributions reported by survey participants amount to 34% of the estimated total contributions by all U.S. corporations. (See Table A on page 11.)

Matched cases—of some of the largest corporations in the United States—were eliminated this year. Many survey respondents had changed their structures—adding or shedding units and product lines. It may be useful, however, to note that a core group of 215 companies participated in 1987 and 1988. These are larger donors, contributing a median donation of $2,194,570.

Many of the restructured companies that were able to respond to the survey lacked complete beneficiary data. Frequently, where separate programs were continued after an acquisition, beneficiary data were available from only one program. Contributions without beneficiary data are in a new category: "Unspecified."

Industry Leaders

Median Contributions as a Percent of U.S. Pretax Income
Food, beverage and tobacco 2.7%
Pharmaceuticals 2.3
Chemicals 1.7
Transportation equipment 1.7
Retail and wholesale trade 1.6

Median Total Contributions ($ Thousands)
Transportation equipment $12,190
Petroleum and gas 10,939
Food, beverage, and tobacco 7,375
Industrial machinery and computers 4,309
Chemicals 3,332

Aggregate Total Contributions ($ Thousands)
Industrial machinery and computers $136,723
Transportation equipment 107,854
Retail and wholesale trade 84,580
Chemicals 67,311
Insurance 64,348

The Top Five Industry Leaders in Corporate Assistance Expenditures

Total Corporate Assistance ($ Millions)
Industrial machinery and computers $93
Food, beverage and tobacco 15
Petroleum and gas 12
Telecommunications 10
Pharmaceuticals 9

Median Corporate Assistance ($ Thousands)
Industrial machinery and computers $5,979
Chemicals 1,024
Telecommunications 719
Printing and publishing 447
Paper and like products 318

Corporate Assistance as Percent of Total Contributions
Industrial machinery and computers 58%
Food, beverage and tobacco 39
Business Services 35
Insurance 16
Utilities 15

The Top Five Industry Leaders in Giving to Health and Human Services

Aggregate Percent of Total Contributions
Utilities 48%
Finance 44
Retail and wholesale trade 41
Insurance 38
Transportation 38

Median Percent of Total Contributions
Utilities 48%
Retail and wholesale trade 47
Electrical machinery (except computers) 41
Food, beverage and tobacco 41
Finance 40

Aggregate Dollar Value of Contributions ($ Millions)
Retail and wholesale trade $61
Industrial machinery and computers 48
Petroleum and gas 43
Transportation equipment 41
Banking 41

Median Dollar Value of Contributions ($ Thousands)
Telecommunications $1,443
Retail and wholesale trade 1,435
Pharmaceuticals 1,144
Petroleum and gas 908
Food, beverage and tobacco .755

The Top Five Industry Leaders in Giving to Education

Aggregate Percent of Total Contributions
Transportation 58%
Utilities 50
Electrical machinery (except computers) 49
Petroleum and gas 48
Industrial machinery and computers 47

Median Percent of Total Contributions
Textile and apparel 52%
Petroleum and gas 42
Chemicals 42
Transportation equipment 38
Electrical machinery (except computers) 38

Aggregate Dollar Value of Contributions ($ Millions)
Industrial machinery and computers $96
Petroleum and gas 85
Transportation equipment 80
Telecommunications 48
Other manufacturing 41

Median Dollar Value of Contributions ($ Thousands)
Pharmaceuticals $184
Telecommunications 144
Chemicals 120
Petroleum and gas 111
Printing and publishing 106

The Top Five Industry Leaders in Giving to Culture and the Arts

Aggregate Percent of Total Contributions
Transportation 19%
Insurance 19
Telecommunications 17
Banking 17
Retail and wholesale trade 14

Median Percent of Total Contributions
Telecommunications 18%
Banking 16
Printing and publishing 15
Finance 13
Insurance 11

Aggregate Dollar Value of Contributions ($ Millions)
Telecommunications $21
Petroleum and gas 20
Industrial machinery and computers 19
Banking 19
Retail and wholesale trade 18

Median Dollar Value of Contributions ($ Thousands)
Telecommunications $852
Printing and publishing 574
Petroleum and gas 378
Finance 284
Transportation equipment 259

The Top Five Industry Leaders in Giving to Civic and Community Activities

Aggregate Percent of Total Contributions
Chemicals 26%
Petroleum and gas 19
Insurance 17
Paper and like products 16
Banking 15

Median Percent of Total Contributions
Textiles and apparel 19
Banking 15
Insurance 15
Retail and wholesale trade 15
Petroleum and gas 15

Aggregate Dollar Value of Contributions ($ Millions)
Pharmaceuticals $29
Petroleum and gas 28
Chemicals 23
Retail and wholesale trade 21
Banking 17

Median Dollar Value of Contributions ($ Thousands)
Pharmaceuticals $790
Finance 618
Telecommunications 459
Printing and publishing 399
Petroleum and gas 326

The Top Five Industry Leaders in Giving to "Other" Group

Aggregate Percent of Total Contributions
Pharmaceuticals 20%
Printing and publishing 18
Industrial machinery and computers 14
Textiles and apparel 11
Business services 9

Median Percent of Total Contributions
Textiles and apparel 15%
Printing and publishing 15
Pharmaceuticals 5
Transportation 4
Business services 3

Aggregate Dollar Value of Contributions ($ Millions)
Pharmaceuticals $30
Industrial machinery and computers 28
Retail and wholesale trade 9
Other manufacturing 9
Banking 8

Median Dollar Value of Contributions ($ Thousands)
Pharmaceuticals $290
Printing and publishing 290
Industrial machinery and computers 173
Finance 139
Telecommunications 90

Chart 1

Current and Constant Dollars, since 1972, of Contributions and Income Before Taxes

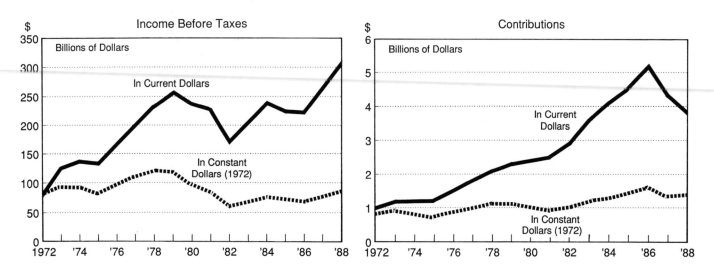

Chart 2

Percentage Change in All Corporate Contributions and Income Before Taxes in Constant Dollars, 1972 to 1988

Note: 1987 and 1988 are based on estimates

Chart 3

Distribution of the Contributions Dollar, 1987 and 1988

Chart 4

Recipients of Corporate Support, 1979 - 1988

1987
$1,658.4 Millions
Reported by 325 Companies

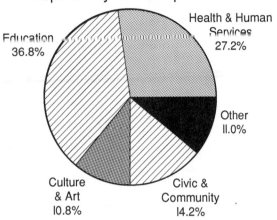

Education 36.8%

Health & Human Services 27.2%

Other 11.0%

Culture & Art 10.8%

Civic & Community 14.2%

1988
$1,645.6 Millions
Reported by 356 Companies

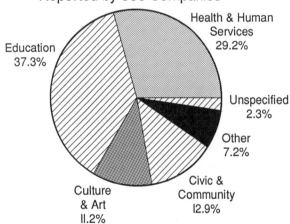

Education 37.3%

Health & Human Services 29.2%

Unspecified 2.3%

Other 7.2%

Culture & Art 11.2%

Civic & Community 12.9%

Health and Human Services

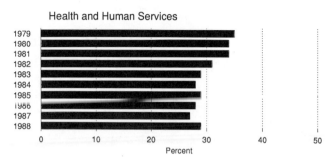

Percent

Education

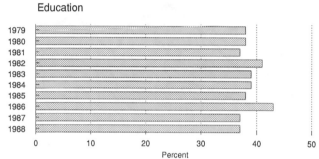

Percent

Culture and Art

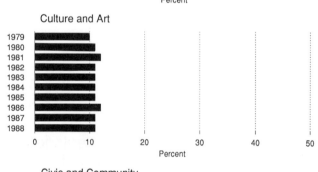

Percent

Civic and Community

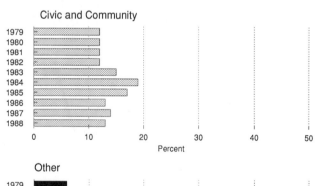

Percent

Other

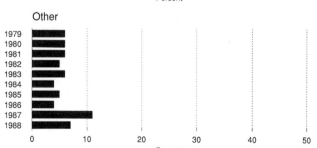

Percent

Note: Unspecified (beneficiaries) in 1988 received 2%

Chart 5A
Health and Human Services Contributions, by Size of Program, Medians

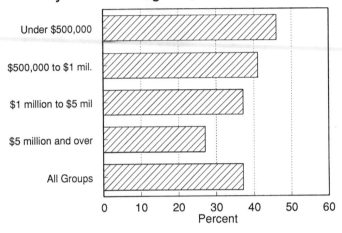

Chart 5B
Education Contributions, by Size of Program, Medians

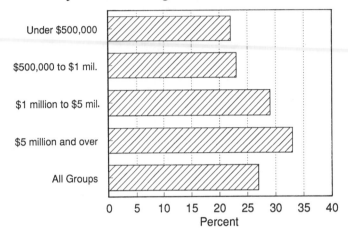

Chart 5C
Culture and Art Contributions, by Size of Program, Medians

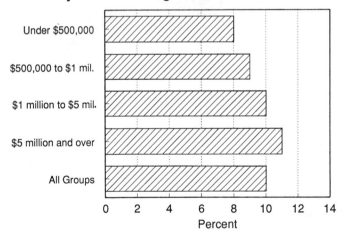

Chart 5D
Civic and Community Contributions, by Size of Program, Medians

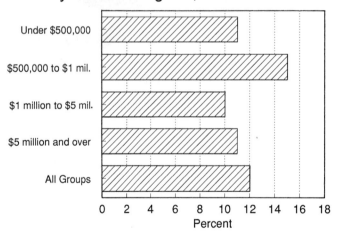

Health and Human Services, Giving to Subcategories

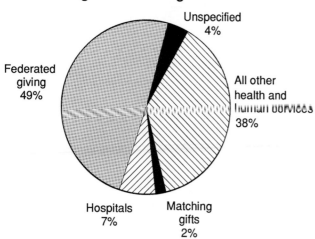

Unspecified
4%

Federated
giving
49%

All other
health and
human services
38%

Hospitals
7%

Matching
gifts
2%

Education, Giving to Subcategories

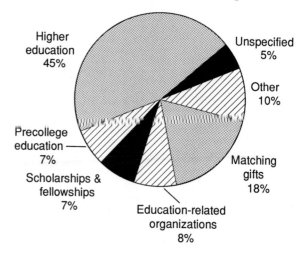

Higher
education
45%

Unspecified
5%

Other
10%

Precollege
education
7%

Scholarships &
fellowships
7%

Education-related
organizations
8%

Matching
gifts
18%

Matching Gifts Contributions, Distribution

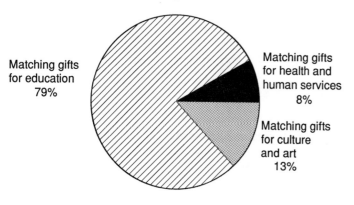

Matching gifts
for education
79%

Matching gifts
for health and
human services
8%

Matching gifts
for culture
and art
13%

Civic and Community Activities, Giving to Subcategories

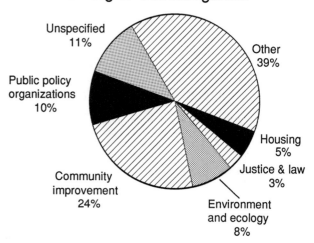

Unspecified
11%

Public policy
organizations
10%

Other
39%

Community
improvement
24%

Housing
5%

Justice & law
3%

Environment
and ecology
8%

Chart 7

Corporate Contributions, Distribution by Industry Sector

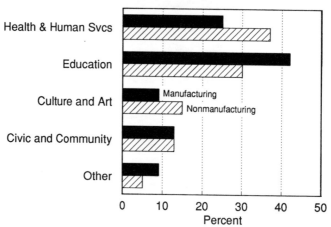

Health & Human Svcs

Education

Culture and Art

Civic and Community

Other

Manufacturing

Nonmanufacturing

0   10   20   30   40   50
Percent

Chart 8

Cash and Noncash Giving
1984 to 1988

%
100
80
60
40
20
0

| 1984 | 1985 | 1986 | 1987 | 1988 |

■ Cash   ▨ Non-Cash

Chart 9

Cash and Noncash Components
of Charitable Contributions, 1988

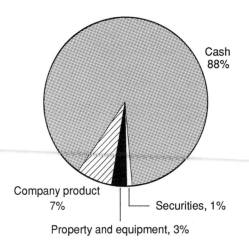

Cash
88%

Company product
7%

Securities, 1%

Property and equipment, 3%

Chart 10

Cash and Noncash Giving, by Industry, 1988

Industry Classification
➡

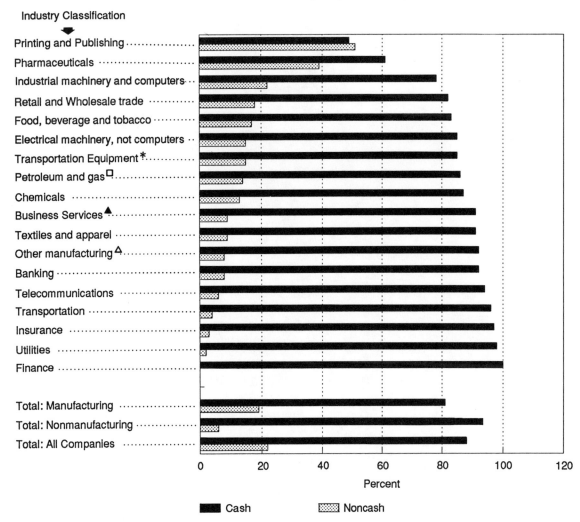

Printing and Publishing ···············
Pharmaceuticals ··············
Industrial machinery and computers ···
Retail and Wholesale trade ··········
Food, beverage and tobacco ········
Electrical machinery, not computers ··
Transportation Equipment * ···········
Petroleum and gas □ ················
Chemicals ·············
Business Services ▲ ·············
Textiles and apparel ············
Other manufacturing △ ············
Banking ·············
Telecommunications ············
Transportation ············
Insurance ·············
Utilities ·············
Finance ·············

Total: Manufacturing ··············
Total: Nonmanufacturing ···········
Total: All Companies ··············

0   20   40   60   80   100   120

Percent

■ Cash   ▦ Noncash

* Includes tire manufacturers.

▲ Includes engineering and construction companies.

△ Includes primary metal industries, fabricated metal products, and stone, clay and glass products.

□ Includes mining companies.

Chart 11

Anticipated Changes in 1989 Budgets, by Industry, Medians

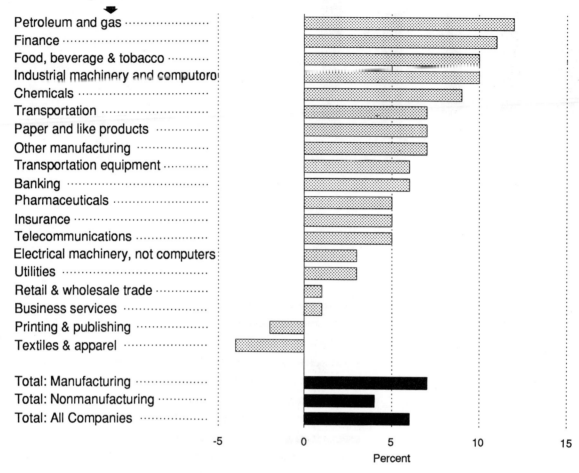

Industry Classification

Petroleum and gas
Finance
Food, beverage & tobacco
Industrial machinery and computers
Chemicals
Transportation
Paper and like products
Other manufacturing
Transportation equipment
Banking
Pharmaceuticals
Insurance
Telecommunications
Electrical machinery, not computers
Utilities
Retail & wholesale trade
Business services
Printing & publishing
Textiles & apparel

Total: Manufacturing
Total: Nonmanufacturing
Total: All Companies

-5   0   5   10   15

Percent

Chart 12

Corporate Assistance as a Percent of Total Contributions, 1984 to 1988

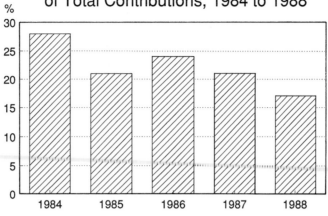

Chart 13

Foundation Giving as a Percent of Total Contributions

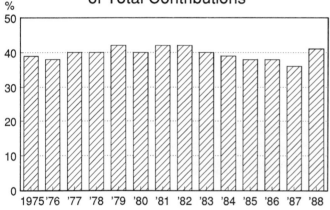

Note: Percentages represent the proportion of the sum of corporate sponsored grants to the sum of total contribution.

Chart 14

Foundations, Relationship of Payouts to Payins

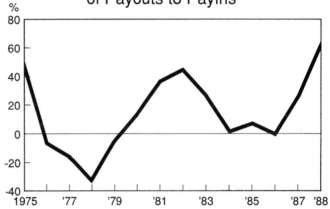

Chart 15

Per Employee Contributions, Medians, 1983 to 1988

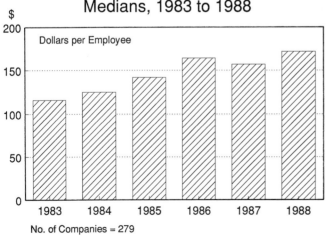

No. of Companies = 279

Chart 16

Per Employee Contributions, 1988
Medians

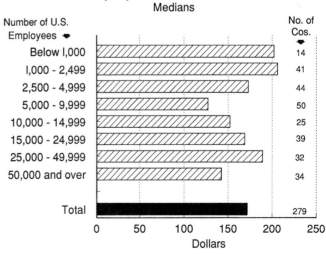

Chart 17

Federated Campaigns Contributions, as a Percentage of Total Giving, by Industry

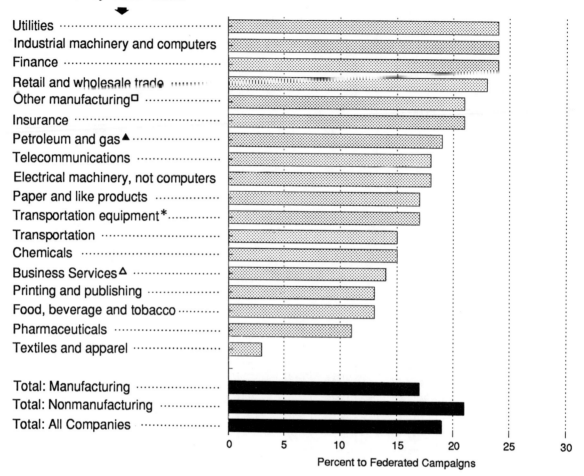

Industry Classification ➡

* Includes tire manufacturers.
▲ Includes mining companies.
△ Includes engineering and construction companies.
□ Includes primary metal industries, fabricated metals and stone, clay and glass products.

Chart 18

Federated Campaigns Contributions,
Per Employee, Median, 1988

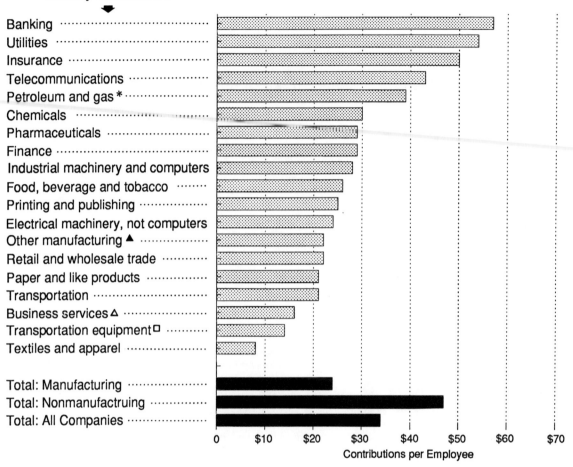

Industry Classification

Banking
Utilities
Insurance
Telecommunications
Petroleum and gas *
Chemicals
Pharmaceuticals
Finance
Industrial machinery and computers
Food, beverage and tobacco
Printing and publishing
Electrical machinery, not computers
Other manufacturing ▲
Retail and wholesale trade
Paper and like products
Transportation
Business services △
Transportation equipment □
Textiles and apparel

Total: Manufacturing
Total: Nonmanufactruing
Total: All Companies

0    $10 $20 $30 $40 $50 $60 $70

Contributions per Employee

* Includes mining companies.
▲ Includes primary metal industries, fabricated metal products and stone, clay and glass products.
△ Includes engineering and construction companies.
□ Includes tire manufacturers.
  Totals include all companies, but detail omits industries with fewer than 4 cases.

Industry Patterns

The tables in this report which employ corporate income data should not be used to assess the overall performance of an industry group participating in this survey. An industry's representation in a given table is determined by how many companies in that industry gave the necessary data for that particular table. Where questionnaire data are incomplete, that company does not appear in the table. Some groups had very few companies reporting this year. The minimum number of companies per table was lowered to 4 companies from 5, although the significance of such results is also diminished.

Another factor causing problems in table comparability is that more companies supply worldwide than U.S. income data (probably because many multinationals do not report their U.S. income separately). Corporations whose income data were unobtainable or unverifiable were not included in tables presenting that information. Thus, Table 1A, which measures contributions as a percent of U.S. income, lists only 51 manufacturing companies, because U.S. income information was not furnished or available for all the participating companies. On the other hand, Table 2, which traces industry donations to specific beneficiary categories, refers to 166—all participating manufacturing companies—because all companies furnished some contributions dollar amount. If companies did not report the specific beneficiary group receiving the funds, their contributions were still counted and reported as "Unspecified."

Table A: All Corporate Contributions and Corporate Income Before and After Taxes[1]

Year	Amount ($ Millions)	Income[4] before Taxes ($ Millions)	As Percent of Income before Taxes	Income[4] after Taxes ($ Millions)	As Percent of Income after Taxes
		Contributions			
1936	$ 30	$ 7,900	0.38%	$ 4,900	0.61%
1937	33	7,900	0.42	5,300	0.62
1938	27	4,100	0.65	2,900	0.93
1939	31	7,200	0.43	5,700	0.54
1940	38	10,000	0.38	7,200	0.53
1941	58	17,900	0.32	10,300	0.56
1942	98	21,700	0.45	10,300	0.95
1943	159	25,300	0.63	11,200	1.42
1944	234	24,200	0.97	11,300	2.07
1945	266	19,800	1.34	9,100	2.92
1946	214	24,800	0.86	15,700	1.36
1947	241	31,800	0.76	20,500	1.18
1948	239	35,600	0.67	23,200	1.03
1949	223	29,200	0.76	19,000	1.17
1950	252	42,900	0.59	25,000	1.01
1951	343	44,500	0.77	21,900	1.57
1952	399	39,600	1.01	20,200	1.98
1953	495	41,200	1.20	20,900	2.37
1954	314	38,700	0.81	21,100	1.49
1955	415	49,200	0.84	27,200	1.53
1956	418	49,600	0.84	27,600	1.51
1957	419	48,100	0.87	26,700	1.57
1958	395	41,900	0.94	22,900	1.72
1959	482	52,600	0.92	28,900	1.67
1960	482	49,800	0.97	27,100	1.78
1961	512	49,700	1.03	26,900	1.90
1962	595	55,000	1.08	31,100	1.91
1963	657	59,600	1.10	33,400	1.97
1964	729	66,500	1.10	38,500	1.89
1965	785	77,200	1.02	46,300	1.70
1966	805	83,000	0.97	49,400	1.63
1967	830	79,700	1.04	47,200	1.76
1968	1,005	88,500	1.13	49,400	2.03
1969	1,055	86,700	1.22	47,200	2.24
1970	797	75,400	1.06	41,300	1.93
1971	865	86,600	1.00	49,000	1.76
1972	1,009	100,600	1.00	58,900	1.71
1973	1,174	125,600	0.93	76,600	1.53
1974	1,200	136,700	0.88	85,100	1.41
1975	1,202	132,100	0.91	81,500	1.47
1976	1,487	166,300	0.89	102,500	1.45
1977	1,791	200,400	0.89	127,400	1.41
1978	2,084	233,500	0.89	150,000	1.39
1979	2,288	257,200	0.89	169,200	1.35
1980	2,359	237,100	0.99	152,300	1.55
1981	2,514	226,500	1.11	145,400	1.73
1982	2,906	169,600	1.71	106,500	2.73
1983	3,627	207,600	1.75	130,400	2.78
1984	4,057	240,000	1.69	146,100	2.78
1985	4,472	224,300	1.99	127,800	3.50
1986	5,179[2]	221,600	2.34	115,300	4.49
1987	4,650(est.)[3]	266,700	1.74	142,000	3.27
1988	$4,800(est.)[3]	$306,800	1.56	$168,900	2.84

[1]Reflects total consolidated corporate income before and after taxes.

[2]The IRS figure is high because it includes some 1987 gifts reported in 1986 to take advantage of the more favorable provisions of the tax law prevailing before the Tax Reform Act of 1986.

[3]From Council for Aid to Education.

[4]The income figures on this table have been adjusted to coincide with recently updated data issued by the Department of Commerce. Thus, some of the figures in the income columns, and the ratios based upon them, will differ slightly from those published here previously.

Note: Figures in this table reflect contributions and income of *all* U.S. corporations. Figures in all other tables in this report are based solely on responses by survey participants.

Sources: Department of Commerce, Internal Revenue Service.

Table 1A: Contributions as a Percent of U.S. Pretax Income, 1988[a]
Grouped by Industry Class[1]

Industrial Classification	Number of Companies	U.S. Pretax Income (Sum) ($ Millions)	Contributions (Sum) ($ Thousands)	U.S. Pretax Income (Median) ($ Thousands)	Contributions (Median) ($ Thousands)	Contributions as a Percent of U.S. Pretax Income (Median)
Chemicals	7	$ 4,576	$ 67,311	$ 194,084	$3,332	1 7%
Electrical machinery (except computers)	5	506	5,450	36,256	426	1.2
Food, beverage and tobacco	2	*	*	*	*	*
Industrial machinery and computers	6	7,729	136,723	395,700	4,309	1.4
Paper and like products	8	2,687	40,674	211,581	1,438	0.7
Petroleum and gas[3]	4	5,482	56,804	1,365,550	10,939	0.7
Pharmaceuticals	4	1,013	30,500	228,310	3,027	2.3
Other manufacturing[4]	8	2,206	24,403	41,972	581	1.1
Printing and publishing	0	(2)				
Textiles and apparel	1	*	*	*	*	*
Transportation equipment[5]	6	9,134	107,854	619,000	12,190	1.7
Total: Manufacturing	51	$ 34,014	$ 469,725	180,000	1,617	1.2
Banking	22	3,665	33,361	75,806	849	1.2
Business services[6]	5	689	2,662	128,000	554	0.5
Finance	2	*	*	*	*	*
Insurance[7]	29	7,449	64,348	138,780	599	1.2
Retail and wholesale trade	7	3,271	84,580	179,100	2,628	1.6
Telecommunications	6	4,235	21,068	562,688	3,180	0.6
Transportation	3	*	*	*	*	*
Utilities	40	10,386	39,853	122,673	598	0.5
Total: Nonmanufacturing	114	$ 31,062	$ 245,872	127,495	781	0.8
Total: All Companies	165	$ 65,075	$ 715,597	137,440	929	0.9

[a]The number of participating corporation within an industry will vary between Tables 1A & 1B. Not all companies isolated their U.S. income, consequently those companies will only appear in the worldwide Table, 1B. Conversely, in some cases, there will be more companies in the U.S. than in the worldwide table, because not all respondents had overseas income.

[1]Loss companies excluded.

[2]Reported only worldwide income.

[3]Includes mining companies.

[4]Includes primary metal industries, fabricated metal products, and stone, clay and glass products.

[5]Includes tire manufacturers.

[6]Includes engineering and construction companies.

[7]Insurance company figures are based on "net gain from operations after dividends to policyholders and before federal income tax, excluding capital gains and losses"— the closest measure to pretax income of corporations generally.

*Industries with fewer than 4 cases are excluded.

Table 1B: Contributions as a Percent of Worldwide Income, 1988[a]
Grouped by Industry Class[1]

Industrial Classification	Number of Companies	Worldwide Pretax Income (Sum) ($ Millions)	Contributions (Sum) ($ Thousands)	Worldwide Pretax Income (Median) ($ Thousands)	Contributions (Median) ($ Thousands)	Contributions as a Percent of Worldwide Pretax Income (Median)
Chemicals	16	$ 19,808	$ 89,465	$ 324,833	$2,222	0.7%
Electrical machinery (except computers)	8	2,302	13,277	227,186	576	0.6
Food, beverage and tobacco	10	4,712	57,576	389,368	4,208	1.0
Industrial machinery and computers	15	20,564	203,551	212,727	2,476	0.9
Paper and like products	12	6,695	52,522	416,005	1,683	0.6
Petroleum and gas[3]	18	29,991	168,703	693,001	5,252	0.5
Pharmaceuticals	14	11,309	145,178	781,170	8,810	1.1
Other manufacturing[4]	24	11,129	96,979	205,650	861	0.8
Printing and publishing	4	1,198	21,325	307,215	4,848	2.3
Textiles and apparel	2	*	*	*	*	*
Transportation equipment[5]	15	20,827	151,573	420,000	8,159	1.1
Total: Manufacturing	138	$128,535	$1,000,149	302,617	2,512	0.8
Banking	13	10,449	69,206	632,800	5,599	0.7
Business services[6]	10	2,423	21,418	137,497	1,284	0.9
Finance	5	3,797	36,877	753,000	3,252	0.7
Insurance[7]	13	4,414	54,909	359,736	916	1.2
Retail and wholesale trade	8	5,806	109,901	472,020	7,229	1.2
Telecommunications	5	7,861	55,045	1,688,200	14,989	0.7
Transportation	2	*	*	*	*	*
Utilities	6	1,025	3,804	112,735	589	0.4
Total: Nonmanufacturing	62	$ 35,775	$ 351,160	421,404	2,867	0.9
Total: All Companies	200	$164,310	$1,351,309	352,868	2,541	0.8

[a]The number of participating corporation within an industry will vary between Tables 1A & 1B. Not all companies isolated their U.S. income, consequently those companies will only appear in the worldwide Table, 1B. Conversely, in some cases, there will be more companies in the U.S. than in the worldwide table, because not all respondents had overseas income.

[1]Loss companies excluded.

[2]Reported only worldwide income.

[3]Includes mining companies.

[4]Includes primary metal industries, fabricated metal products, and stone, clay and glass products.

[5]Includes tire manufacturers.

[6]Includes engineering and construction companies.

[7]Insurance company figures are based on "net gain from operations after dividends to policyholders and before federal income tax, excluding capital gains and losses"—the closest measure to pretax income of corporations generally.

*Industries with fewer than 4 cases are excluded.

Table 2: Beneficiaries of Corporate Support, 1985 to 1988

	1988 356 Companies		1987 325 Companies		1986 370 Companies		1985 436 Companies	
	Thousands of Dollars	% of Total	Thousands of Dollars	% of Total	Thousands of Dollars	% of Total	Thousands of Dollars	% of Total
Health and Human Services								
Federated giving	$ 234,045	14.2%	$ 203,582	12.3%	$ 225,944	13.5		
Hospitals	35,249	2.1	31,071	1.9	27,620	1.6		
Matching gifts for health and human services	10,283	0.6	4,439	0.3	5,527	0.3		
All other health and human services	181,406	11.0	146,441	8.8	167,320	10.0		
Subcategories unspecified	10,200	1.2	64,982	3.9	42,239	2.5		
Total health and human services	$ 480,191	29.2	$ 450,515	27.2%	$ 468,650	28.0%	$ 494,109	29.2%
Education								
Higher education	275,545	16.7	290,873	17.5	400,405	23.9		
Precollege education	41,591	2.5	25,232	1.5	30,873	1.8		
Scholarships and fellowships	43,681	2.7	39,934	2.4	37,145	2.2		
Education-related organizations	55,874	3.4	33,779	2.0	30,688	1.8		
Matching gifts for education	108,190	6.6	108,257	6.5	107,436	6.4		
Other	61,604	3.7	64,951	3.9	44,932	2.7		
Subcategories unspecified	27,565	1.7	47,121	2.8	66,504	4.0		
Total education	$ 614,050	37.3	$ 610,146	36.8%	$ 717,983	42.9%	$ 650,005	38.3%
Culture and Art								
Matching gifts for culture and art	18,209	1.1	13,601	0.8	14,782	0.9		
All other culture and art	158,147	9.6	151,533	9.1	144,953	8.7		
Subcategories unspecified	7,237	0.4	13,471	0.8	39,019	2.3		
Total culture and art	183,592	11.2	$ 178,605	10.8%	$ 198,754	11.9%	$ 187,536	11.1%
Civic and Community								
Public policy organizations	20,918	1.3	22,004	1.3	15,711	0.9		
Community improvement	51,335	3.1	53,356	3.2	72,622	4.3		
Environment and ecology	17,349	1.1	44,026	2.7	35,953	2.1		
Justice and law	5,711	0.3	6,808	0.4	7,033	0.4		
Housing	9,876	0.6	6,395	0.4	8,237	0.5		
Other	84,275	5.1	61,956	3.7	35,155	2.1		
Subcategories unspecified	22,647	1.4	41,580	2.5	45,678	2.7		
Total civic and community	$ 212,111	12.9	$ 236,124	14.2%	$ 220,479	13.2%	$ 279,508	16.5%
Other								
Total other	$ 118,414	7.2	$ 182,992	11.0%	$ 68,119	4.1%	$ 83,549	4.9%
Unspecified	$ 37,331	2.3						
Grand total	$1,645,689	100.0	$1,658,382	100.0%	$1,673,985	100.0%	$1,694,707	100.0%

The data from previous years in Table 2 has been restated to correspond to the combined subcategories introduced in 1987.

Subcategories may not add to totals due to rounding.

Table 3A: Health and Human Services Beneficiaries of Company Support, 1988—Companies Grouped by Industry Class

Industrial Classification	Number of Companies	Total Contributions ($ Thousands)	Federated Giving ($ Thousands)	Percent of Industry Contribution	Hospitals ($ Thousands)	Percent of Industry Contribution	Matching Gifts ($ Thousands)	Percent of Industry Contribution	All Other Health and Human Services ($ Thousands)	Percent of Industry Contribution	Unspecified ($ Thousands)	Percent of Industry Contribution	Total Health and Human Services ($ Thousands)	Percent of Industry Contribution
Chemicals	16	$ 89,465	$ 9,164	10.2%	$ 1,125	1.3%	$ 73	0.1%	$ 4,814	5.4%	$ 2,496	2.8%	$ 17,672	19.8%
Electrical machinery (except computers)	10	22,149	2,987	13.5	308	1.4	0	0.0	1,661	7.5	1,016	4.6	5,972	27.0
Food, beverage and tobacco	12	58,830	4,429	7.5	828	1.4	347	0.6	10,682	18.2	2,064	3.5	18,350	31.2
Industrial machinery and computers	16	203,979	29,228	14.3	4,054	2.0	5,224	2.6	9,358	4.6	0	0.0	47,864	23.5
Paper and like products	15	53,524	7,082	13.2	407	0.8	211	0.4	8,255	15.4	0	0.0	15,954	29.8
Petroleum and gas[1]	23	178,522	21,305	11.9	2,724	1.5	823	0.5	16,691	9.3	1,318	0.7	42,861	24.0
Pharmaceuticals	17	149,695	13,869	9.3	8,296	5.5	188	0.1	17,082	11.4	1,021	0.7	40,456	27.0
Other manufacturing[2]	30	99,938	14,608	14.6	2,559	2.6	216	0.2	6,964	7.0	756	0.8	25,103	25.1
Printing and publishing	6	36,892	2,924	7.9	173	0.5	2	0.0	852	2.3	0	0.0	3,950	10.7
Textiles and apparel	4	3,711	207	5.6	2	0.1	0	0.0	275	7.4	95	2.6	579	15.6
Transportation equipment[3]	20	158,933	23,084	14.5	3,929	2.5	40	0.0	13,833	8.7	46	0.0	40,932	25.8
Total: Manufacturing	169	1,055,638	128,887	12.2	24,405	2.3	7,124	0.7	90,467	8.6	8,812	0.8	259,693	24.6
Banking	43	112,972	20,106	17.8	3,132	2.8	810	0.7	15,923	14.1	606	0.5	40,577	35.9
Business services[4]	18	32,426	3,625	11.2	421	1.3	652	2.0	4,201	13.0	1,834	5.7	10,733	33.1
Finance	6	38,231	8,548	22.4	950	2.5	169	0.4	7,289	19.1	0	0.0	16,956	44.4
Insurance	39	80,882	15,032	18.6	1,670	2.1	473	0.6	12,048	14.9	1,548	1.9	30,771	38.0
Retail and wholesale trade	15	147,529	24,305	16.5	1,750	1.2	119	0.1	34,623	23.5	62	0.0	60,859	41.3
Telecommunications	12	119,604	20,795	17.4	1,389	1.2	292	0.2	6,634	5.5	4,907	4.1	34,017	28.4
Transportation	7	14,311	1,799	12.6	21	0.1	52	0.4	3,533	24.7	35	0.2	5,440	38.0
Utilities	47	44,096	10,947	24.8	1,511	3.4	593	1.3	6,688	15.2	1,406	3.2	21,145	48.0
Total: Nonmanufacturing	187	590,051	105,157	17.8	10,844	1.8	3,160	0.5	90,939	15.4	10,398	1.8	220,498	37.4
Total: All Companies	356	$1,645,689	$ 234,044	14.2	$ 35,249	2.1	$ 10,284	0.6	$ 181,406	11.0	$ 19,208	1.2	$ 480,191	29.2

[1]Includes mining companies.
[2]Includes primary metal industries, fabricated metal products, and stone, clay and glass products.
[3]Includes tire manufacturers.
[4]Includes engineering and construction companies.
Details in a row may not add to total due to rounding.

Table 3B: Education Beneficiaries of Company Support, 1988—Companies Grouped by Industry Class

Industrial Classification	Higher Education		Precollege Education		Scholarships and Fellowships		Education Related Organizations	
	($ Thousands)	Percent of Industry Contribution	($ Thousands)	Percent of Industry Contribution	($ Thousands)	Percent of Industry Contribution	($ Thousands)	Percent of Industry Contribution
Chemicals	$ 19,079	21.3%	$ 1,851	2.1%	$ 1,537	1.7%	$ 2,622	2.9
Electrical machinery (except computers)	6,284	28.4	461	2.1	201	1.0	347	1.6
Food, beverage and tobacco	5,061	8.6	481	0.8	493	0.8	1,924	3.3
Industrial machinery and computers	57,631	28.3	4,748	2.3	7,211	3.5	6,554	3.2
Paper and like products	12,218	22.8	1,092	2.0	877	1.6	4,999	9.3
Petroleum and gas[1]	31,704	17.8	6,771	3.8	4,507	2.5	8,714	4.9
Pharmaceuticals	17,393	11.6	1,284	0.9	3,879	2.6	5,854	3.9
Other manufacturing[2]	22,281	22.3	3,651	3.7	3,029	3.0	2,476	2.5
Printing and publishing	1,552	4.2	4,415	12.0	759	2.1	633	1.7
Textiles and apparel	1,283	34.6	154	4.1	59	1.6	143	3.9
Transportation equipment[3]	33,991	21.4	5,032	3.2	4,786	3.0	5,192	3.3
Total: Manufacturing	208,477	19.7	29,940	2.8	27,528	2.6	39,458	3.7
Banking	9,095	8.1	2,075	1.8	968	0.9	3,853	3.4
Business services[4]	3,151	9.7	469	1.4	2,531	7.8	508	1.6
Finance	2,498	6.5	3,012	7.9	1,852	4.8	753	2.0
Insurance	9,085	11.2	1,271	1.6	1,344	1.7	2,933	3.6
Retail and wholesale trade	7,581	5.1	2,979	2.0	6,039	4.1	3,471	2.4
Telecommunications	27,797	23.2	962	0.8	2,517	2.1	4,006	3.3
Transportation	3,087	21.6	58	0.4	317	2.2	132	0.9
Utilities	4,774	10.8	825	1.9	585	1.3	760	1.7
Total: Nonmanufacturing	67,068	11.4	11,651	2.0	16,153	2.7	16,416	2.8
Total: All Companies	$275,545	16.7	$41,591	2.5	$43,681	2.7	$55,874	3.4

[1]Includes mining companies.
[2]Includes primary metal industries, fabricated metal products, and stone, clay and glass products.
[3]Includes tire manufacturers.
[4]Includes engineering and construction companies.
Details in a row may not add to total due to rounding.

Matching Gifts		Other		Unspecified		Total Education	
($ Thousands)	Percent of Industry Contribution	($ Thousands)	Percent of Industry Contribution	($ Thousands)	Percent of Industry Contribution	($ Thousands)	Percent of Industry Contribution
$ 3,696	4.1%	$ 311	0.3%	$ 9,048	10.1%	$ 38,143	42.6
1,310	5.9	0	0.0	1,965	8.9	10,759	48.6
1,889	3.2	524	0.9	3,202	5.4	13,574	23.1
18,900	9.3	900	0.4	0	0.0	95,944	47.0
2,020	3.8	389	0.5	0	0.0	21,495	40.2
21,384	12.0	9,135	5.1	3,166	1.8	85,381	47.8
7,812	5.2	3,215	2.1	0	0.0	39,435	26.3
5,196	5.2	4,194	4.2	333	0.3	41,161	41.2
2,276	6.2	58	0.2	0	0.0	9,693	26.3
516	13.9	0	0.0	0	0.0	2,155	58.1
8,383	5.3	22,771	14.3	0	0.0	80,155	50.4
73,382	7.0	41,397	3.9	17,713	1.7	437,895	41.5
7,722	6.8	3,106	2.7	138	0.1	26,956	23.9
5,326	16.4	1,222	3.8	420	1.3	13,628	42.0
2,421	6.3	0	0.0	0	0.0	10,536	27.6
6,311	7.8	849	1.0	1,725	2.1	23,517	29.1
4,151	2.8	13,663	9.3	960	0.7	38,844	26.3
6,734	5.6	875	0.7	5,112	4.3	48,003	40.1
861	6.0	0	0.0	145	1.0	4,601	32.2
1,282	2.9	492	1.1	1,351	3.1	10,070	22.8
34,808	5.9	20,207	3.4	9,852	1.7	176,155	29.9
$108,190	6.6	$61,604	3.7	$27,565	1.7	$614,050	37.3

Table 3C: Culture and Art Beneficiaries of Company Support, 1988—Companies Grouped by Industry Class

Industrial Classification	Matching Gifts ($ Thousands)	Percent of Industry Contribution	All Other Culture and Art ($ Thousands)	Percent of Industry Contribution	Unspecified ($ Thousands)	Percent of Industry Contribution	Total Culture and Art ($ Thousands)	Percent of Industry Contribution
Chemicals	$ 383	0.4%	$ 4,896	5.5%	$ 518	0.6%	$ 5,798	6.5
Electrical machinery (except computers)	272	1.2	1,407	6.4	138	0.6	1,817	8.2
Food, beverage and tobacco	227	0.4	5,387	9.2	482	0.8	6,097	10.4
Industrial machinery and computers	5,430	2.7	14,046	6.9	0	0.0	19,476	9.5
Paper and like products	231	0.4	4,165	7.8	0	0.0	4,396	8.2
Petroleum and gas[1]	2,004	1.1	17,434	9.8	517	0.3	19,956	11.2
Pharmaceuticals	750	0.5	7,457	5.0	0	0.0	8,207	5.5
Other manufacturing[2]	1,088	1.1	11,599	11.6	171	0.2	12,858	12.9
Printing and publishing	821	2.2	2,392	6.5	0	0.0	3,213	8.7
Textiles and apparel	0	0.0	32	0.9	82	2.2	114	3.1
Transportation equipment[3]	1,153	0.7	15,892	10.0	0	0.0	17,045	10.7
Total: Manufacturing	12,359	1.2	84,707	8.0	1,911	0.2	98,977	9.4
Banking	2,660	2.4	15,543	13.8	661	0.6	18,864	16.7
Business services[4]	0	0.0	2,256	7.0	218	0.7	2,474	7.6
Finance	203	0.5	6,275	16.4	0	0.0	6,479	16.9
Insurance	354	0.4	10,324	12.8	558	0.7	11,236	13.9
Retail and wholesale trade	313	0.2	16,715	11.3	844	0.6	17,872	12.1
Telecommunications	1,953	1.6	16,267	13.6	2,330	1.9	20,549	17.2
Transportation	214	1.5	2,444	17.1	13	0.1	2,671	18.7
Utilities	153	0.3	3,616	8.2	705	1.6	4,473	10.1
Total: Nonmanufacturing	5,850	1.0	73,440	12.4	5,328	0.9	84,618	14.3
Total: All Companies	$ 18,209	1.1	$158,147	9.6	$ 7,237	0.4	$183,595	11.2

[1]Includes mining companies.
[2]Includes primary metal industries, fabricated metal products, and stone, clay and glass products.
[3]Includes tire manufacturers.
[4]Includes engineering and construction companies.
Details in a row may not add to total due to rounding.

Table 3D: Civic and Community Beneficiaries of Company Support, 1988—Companies Grouped by Industry Class

Industrial Classification	Public Policy Organizations ($ Thousands)	Percent of Industry Contribution	Community Improvement ($ Thousands)	Percent of Industry Contribution	Environment and Ecology ($ Thousands)	Percent of Industry Contribution	Justice and Law ($ Thousands)	Percent of Industry Contribution
Chemicals	$ 599	0.7%	$ 1,072	1.2%	$ 8,246	9.2%	$ 257	0.3
Electrical machinery (except computers)	39	0.2	792	3.6	33	0.1	50	0.2
Food, beverage and tobacco	538	0.9	1,708	2.9	800	1.5	466	0.8
Industrial machinery and computers	1,475	0.7	3,326	1.6	489	0.2	742	0.4
Paper and like products	163	0.3	1,653	3.1	337	0.6	51	0.1
Petroleum and gas[1]	4,807	2.7	6,205	3.5	3,239	1.8	1,064	0.6
Pharmaceuticals	3,513	2.3	3,244	2.2	396	0.3	360	0.2
Other manufacturing[2]	1,213	1.2	5,536	5.5	967	1.0	317	0.3
Printing and publishing	152	0.4	763	2.1	36	0.1	63	0.2
Textiles and apparel	4	0.1	35	0.9	0	0.0	0	0.0
Transportation equipment[3]	2,367	1.5	3,769	2.4	986	0.6	467	0.3
Total: Manufacturing	14,870	1.4	28,103	2.7	15,624	1.5	3,837	0.4
Banking	1,615	1.4	4,270	3.8	745	0.7	293	0.3
Business services[4]	170	0.5	1,410	4.3	162	0.5	43	0.1
Finance	769	2.0	755	2.0	0	0.0	29	0.1
Insurance	1,421	1.8	3,451	4.3	243	0.3	715	0.9
Retail and wholesale trade	965	0.7	9,856	6.7	153	0.1	266	0.2
Telecommunications	695	0.6	1,632	1.4	201	0.2	409	0.3
Transportation	144	1.0	108	0.8	6	0.0	0	0.0
Utilities	268	0.6	1,750	4.0	215	0.5	119	0.3
Total: Nonmanufacturing	6,047	1.0	23,232	3.9	1,725	0.3	1,874	0.3
Total: All Companies	$ 20,917	1.5	$51,335	3.1	$17,349	1.1	$ 5,711	0.3

[1]Includes mining companies.
[2]Includes primary metal industries, fabricated metal products, and stone, clay and glass products.
[3]Includes tire manufacturers.
[4]Includes engineering and construction companies.
Details in a row may not add to total due to rounding.

Housing		Other		Unspecified		Total Civic and Community	
($ Thousands)	Percent of Industry Contribution	($ Thousands)	Percent of Industry Contribution	($ Thousands)	Percent of Industry Contribution	($ Thousands)	Percent of Industry Contribution
$ 274	0.3%	$ 3,831	4.3%	$ 8,946	10.0%	$23,225	26.0
182	0.8	95	0.4	395	1.8	1,587	7.2
422	0.7	2,172	3.7	288	0.5	6,490	11.0
24	0.0	7,011	3.4	0	0.0	13,068	6.4
87	0.2	4,386	8.2	201	0.4	6,878	12.9
1,438	0.8	11,125	6.2	342	0.2	28,219	15.8
826	0.6	19,335	12.9	1,084	0.7	28,758	19.2
804	0.8	3,170	3.2	207	0.2	12,221	12.2
18	0.0	1,144	3.1	0	0.0	2,176	5.9
0	0.0	216	5.8	221	6.0	476	12.8
374	0.2	5,818	3.7	0	0.0	13,781	8.7
4,449	0.4	58,311	5.5	11,684	1.1	136,879	13.0
2,573	2.3	6,381	5.6	718	0.6	16,595	14.7
45	0.1	751	2.3	151	0.5	2,732	8.4
1,132	3.0	1,282	3.4	0	0.0	3,967	10.4
1,048	1.3	5,144	6.4	1,917	2.4	13,939	17.2
252	0.2	6,325	4.3	2,768	1.9	20,585	14.0
235	0.2	2,829	2.4	4,338	3.6	10,340	8.6
21	0.1	409	2.9	104	0.7	793	5.5
121	0.3	2,843	6.4	967	2.2	6,284	14.3
5,427	0.9	25,964	4.4	10,963	1.9	75,235	12.8
$ 9,876	0.6	$84,275	5.1	$ 22,647	1.4	$212,111	12.9

Table 3E: Beneficiaries of Company Support, 1988—Companies Grouped by Industry Class

Industrial Classification	Total Other		Unspecified	
	($ Thousands)	Percent of Industry Contribution	($ Thousands)	Percent of Industry Contribution
Chemicals...	$ 4,621	5.2%	$ 5	0.0
Electrical machinery (except computers)	492	2.2	1,524	6.9
Food, beverage and tobacco............................	1,422	2.4	12,898	21.9
Industrial machinery and computers......................	27,627	10.5	U	U.U
Paper and like products..............	2,364	4.4	2,438	4.6
Petroleum and gas[1]	2,104	1.2	0	0.0
Pharmaceuticals..	29,774	19.9	3,064	2.0
Other manufacturing[2]...................................	8,529	8.5	67	0.1
Printing and publishing	6,739	18.3	11,122	30.1
Textiles and apparel....................................	388	10.5	0	0.0
Transportation equipment[3].............................	6,004	3.8	1,016	0.6
Total: Manufacturing	90,064	8.5	32,134	3.0
Banking...	7,704	6.8	2,278	2.0
Business services[4]	2,838	8.8	21	0.1
Finance	286	0.7	7	0.0
Insurance	1,399	1.7	20	0.0
Retail and wholesale trade	9,369	6.4	0	0.0
Telecommunications....................................	4,070	3.4	2,625	2.2
Transportation	766	5.4	40	0.3
Utilities	1,917	4.3	206	0.5
Total: Nonmanufacturing	28,349	4.8	5,197	0.9
Total: All Companies	$118,413	7.2	$ 37,331	2.3

[1]Includes mining companies.
[2]Includes primary metal industries, fabricated metal products, and stone, clay and glass products.
[3]Includes tire manufacturers.
[4]Includes engineering and construction companies.
Details in a row may not add to total due to rounding.

Table 4: Cash and Noncash Giving, by Industry, 1988 [a]

Industry Classification	Number of Companies	Total Contributions Cash and Noncash ($ Thousands)	Cash as a Percent of Total Contributions	Securities as a Percent of Total Contributions	Company Product as a Percent of Total Contributions	Property and Equipment as a Percent of Total Contributions
Chemicals	16	$ 89,465	87%	0%	1%	12%
Electrical machinery (except computers)	10	22,150	85	0	15	1
Food, beverage and tobacco	12	58,706	83	0	18	*
Industrial machinery and computers ...	16	203,979	78	0	13	1
Paper and like products	15	52,674	70	0	30	2
Petroleum and gas[1]	21	158,439	86	0	2	1
Pharmaceuticals	17	149,695	61	0	36	2
Other manufacturing[2]	29	99,833	92	0	*	7
Printing and publishing	6	36,892	49	0	50	1
Textiles and apparel	4	3,711	91	0	5	4
Transportation equipment[3]	20	157,916	85	0	2	17
Total: Manufacturing	166	$1,033,460	81%	0%	12%	5%
Banking	41	102,651	92	0	*	*
Business services[3]	17	31,603	91	0	6	*
Finance	6	38,231	100	0	0	9
Insurance	37	80,282	97	2	*	1
Retail and wholesale trade	15	147,529	82	0	8	6
Telecommunications	12	119,604	94	0	6	*
Transportation	7	14,311	96	0	3	2
Utilities	46	44,000	98	0	*	2
Total: Nonmanufacturing	181	$ 578,211	94%	2%	2%	2%
Total: All Companies	347	$1,611,671	88%	1%	7%	3%

[1]Includes mining companies.

[2]Includes primary metal industries, fabricated metal products, and stone, clay and glass products.

[3]Includes tire manufacturers.

[4]Includes engineering and construction companies.

*Less than 1 percent.

[a]Total may not add to 100 percent due to rounding.

Table 5: 75 Top Donors: Cash and Noncash Giving, 1988

Company Rank	Total Contributions (dollars)	Cash	Cash as % Of Total	Securities	Securities as % Of Total	Company Product	Company Product as % Of Total	Property & Equipment	Property & Equipment as % Of Total
1	$74,965,035	$67,370,930	90%	$0	0%	$ 6,535,122	9%	$ 1,059,183	1%
2	52,345,196	50,645,196	97	0	0	0	0	1,698,000	3
3	50,916,000	33,711,000	66	0	0	0	0	17,205,000	34
4	47,411,026	34,757,011	73	0	0	6,340,138	13	313,877	1
5	43,491,206	36,533,180	84	0	0	6,958,026	16	0	0
6	34,684,591	34,684,591	100	0	0	0	0	0	0
7	34,335,901	26,335,901	77	0	0	0	0	8,000,000	23
8	34,244,678	24,370,872	71	0	0	693,020	2	9,180,786	27
9	30,311,000	14,311,000	47	0	0	16,000,000	53	0	0
10	29,864,949	25,671,018	86	0	0	192,303	1	4,001,628	13
11	29,089,521	13,296,360	46	0	0	15,466,043	53	327,118	1
12	27,628,677	10,031,035	36	0	0	1,597,642	6	0	0
13	26,061,591	9,389,885	36	0	0	16,671,706	64	0	0
14	23,725,000	16,430,000	69	0	0	7,295,000	31	0	0
15	22,888,549	22,739,696	99	0	0	0	0	148,853	1
16	21,667,769	14,667,769	68	0	0	0	0	7,000,000	32
17	20,775,341	16,579,845	80	0	0	2,849,922	14	1,345,574	7
18	20,138,000	20,138,000	100	0	0	0	0	0	0
19	19,962,699	0	0	0	0	0	0	0	0
20	19,791,515	18,645,769	94	0	0	265,762	1	879,984	5
21	18,942,715	18,942,715	100	0	0	0	0	0	0
22	18,636,818	18,636,818	100	0	0	0	0	0	0
23	18,326,369	8,129,929	44	0	0	10,100,485	55	95,955	1
24	17,365,792	17,365,792	100	0	0	0	0	0	0
25	17,000,000	17,000,000	100	0	0	0	0	0	0
26	16,839,000	16,839,000	100	0	0	0	0	0	0
27	15,589,448	15,239,448	98	0	0	150,000	1	200,000	1
28	15,417,412	4,385,397	28	0	0	10,712,398	70	319,617	2
29	15,368,288	15,368,288	100	0	0	0	0	0	0
30	15,146,000	15,146,000	100	0	0	0	0	0	0
31	15,098,426	15,098,426	100	0	0	0	0	0	0
32	15,024,198	14,498,668	97	0	0	0	0	525,530	4
33	14,989,000	14,989,000	100	0	0	0	0	0	0
34	14,121,000	10,121,000	72	0	0	4,000,000	28	0	0
35	12,259,835	6,210,796	51	0	0	6,049,039	49	0	0
36	11,993,524	3,019,965	25	0	0	8,973,559	75	0	0
37	11,668,965	7,544,242	65	0	0	826,362	7	3,298,361	28
38	11,644,317	7,398,329	64	0	0	425,988	37	0	0
39	11,630,400	11,630,400	100	0	0	0	0	0	0
40	11,611,565	11,611,565	100	0	0	0	0	0	0
41	11,436,722	8,506,222	74	0	0	2,800,000	25	130,500	1
42	11,409,000	11,409,000	100	0	0	0	0	0	0
43	11,328,750	11,328,750	100	0	0	0	0	0	0
44	11,100,426	11,100,426	100	0	0	0	0	0	0
45	11,032,221	11,032,221	100	0	0	0	0	0	0
46	10,891,818	10,891,818	100	0	0	0	0	0	0
47	10,817,085	10,817,085	100	0	0	0	0	0	0
48	10,702,208	10,702,208	100	0	0	0	0	0	0
49	10,619,279	10,619,279	100	0	0	0	0	0	0
50	10,455,332	10,435,248	100	0	0	18,584	*	1,500	*

Total in a row may not add to 100 due to rounding.

*Less than 1 percent.

Total row does not add up to 100% because 1 company did not give details or breakdown of their cash and noncash contributions but only reported the total.

Table 5: 75 Top Donors: Cash and Noncash Giving, 1988 (continued)

Company Rank	Total Contributions (dollars)	Cash	Cash as % Of Total	Securities	Securities as % Of Total	Company Product	Company Product as % Of Total	Property & Equipment	Property & Equipment as % Of Total
51	10,300,250	2,600,250	25	0	0	7,700,000	75	0	0
52	10,198,285	8,207,296	80	0	0	1,990,989	20	0	0
53	9,835,000	9,835,000	100	0	0	0	0	0	0
54	9,604,562	9,604,562	100	0	0	0	0	0	0
55	9,322,470	9,322,470	100	0	0	0	0	0	0
56	9,281,336	9,281,336	100	0	0	0	0	0	0
57	8,860,300	8,632,565	97	0	0	0	0	227,735	3
58	8,762,730	8,569,415	98	0	0	193,315	2	0	0
59	8,573,754	8,573,754	100	0	0	0	0	0	0
60	8,330,599	8,330,599	100	0	0	0	0	0	0
61	8,222,587	8,222,587	100	0	0	0	0	0	0
62	8,158,855	8,158,855	100	0	0	0	0	0	0
63	8,039,734	8,039,734	100	0	0	0	0	0	0
64	7,747,772	7,747,772	100	0	0	0	0	0	0
65	7,411,618	7,411,618	100	0	0	0	0	0	0
66	7,220,000	5,220,000	72	0	0	200,000	28	0	0
67	6,862,143	6,808,924	99	0	0	0	0	53,219	1
68	6,760,000	6,760,000	100	0	0	0	0	0	0
69	6,630,000	6,564,199	99	0	0	65,881	1	0	0
70	6,290,881	6,290,881	100	0	0	0	0	0	0
71	5,984,000	5,984,000	100	0	0	0	0	0	0
72	5,716,275	5,716,275	100	0	0	0	0	0	0
73	5,662,829	5,662,829	100	0	0	0	0	0	0
74	5,598,940	5,598,940	100	0	0	0	0	0	0
75	5,326,587	5,326,587	100	0	0	0	0	0	0
Total	$1,267,463,664	$1,028,797,541	82%	0	0	$140,691,284	12%	$56,012,420	5%

Table 6: Beneficiaries of the 75 Top Donors, 1988

Company Rank	Total Contributions (Dollars)	Health and Human Services	Education	Culture and Art	Civic and Community	Other
1	$74,965,035	29%	51%	11%	5%	5%
2	52,343,196	20	30	10	6	35
3	50,916,000	20	67	3	7	2
4	47,411,026	37	30	8	9	15
5	43,491,206	21	54	14	6	5
6	34,684,591	12	61	11	16	*
7	34,335,901	05	1L	8	17	1
8	34,244,678	15	43	5	34	4
9	30,311,000	11	28	2	59	0
10	29,864,949	27	33	20	14	7
11	29,089,521	28	50	5	14	2
12	27,628,677	20	44	11	15	9
13	26,061,591	16	70	3	*	10
14	23,725,000	39	28	9	5	19
15	22,888,549	21	47	7	22	4
16	21,667,769	15	43	5	6	32
17	20,775,341	38	33	13	15	1
18	20,138,000	24	48	16	9	2
19	19,962,699	21	63	7	8	1
20	19,791,515	10	44	2	44	*
21	18,942,715	35	30	27	8	0
22	18,636,818	33	33	19	16	*
23	18,326,369	17	15	7	8	53
24	17,365,792	27	5	45	22	1
25	17,000,000	21	47	9	22	1
26	16,839,000	32	42	9	17	0
27	15,589,448	60	17	5	15	3
28	15,417,412	7	8	6	6	2
29	15,368,288	15	50	16	19	0
30	15,146,000	32	42	17	9	*
31	15,098,426	33	48	13	6	*
32	15,024,198	35	30	6	23	6
33	14,989,900	39	26	25	3	8
34	14,121,000	16	43	1	11	30
35	12,259,835	8	7	10	3	0
36	11,993,524	10	10	2	4	75
37	11,668,965	62	17	6	12	2
38	11,644,317	61	22	6	3	8
39	11,630,400	32	31	5	24	7
40	11,611,565	27	35	13	2	24
41	11,436,722	23	56	11	10	*
42	11,409,000	20	50	20	7	3
43	11,328,750	54	25	9	10	1
44	11,100,426	36	33	5	26	1
45	11,032,221	69	18	3	8	1
46	10,891,818	26	31	22	17	4
47	10,817,085	38	25	18	16	3
48	10,702,208	26	41	13	20	0
49	10,619,279	19	30	20	2	2
50	10,455,332	27	45	12	14	2

Total in a row may not add to 100 percent due to rounding.

*Less than 1 percent.

n.a. = Not available.

Table 6: Beneficiaries of the 75 Top Donors, 1988 (continued)

Company Rank	Total Contributions (Dollars)	Health and Human Services	Education	Culture and Arts	Civic and Community	Other
51	10,300,250	3	46	5	1	45
52	10,198,285	45	25	13	17	1
53	9,835,000	58	17	18	7	0
54	9,604,562	39	19	29	14	0
55	9,322,270	27	29	9	7	0
56	9,281,336	40	35	9	4	12
57	8,860,300	38	33	22	3	4
58	8,762,730	28	32	13	10	1
59	8,573,754	30	33	21	16	0
60	8,330,599	28	34	23	15	0
61	8,222,587	33	38	13	4	12
62	8,158,855	26	51	14	7	3
63	8,039,734	45	29	17	6	2
64	7,747,772	32	17	13	10	28
65	7,411,618	25	30	16	19	10
66	7,220,000	16	62	10	10	2
67	6,862,143	35	20	28	15	2
68	6,760,000	36	29	13	22	0
69	6,630,000	27	37	13	16	8
70	6,290,881	26	36	20	17	2
71	5,984,000	0	100	0	0	0
72	5,716,275	21	57	7	9	5
73	5,662,829	15	17	59	8	1
74	5,598,940	39	13	12	10	26
75	5,326,587	17	60	10	6	7

Total in a row may not add to 100 percent due to rounding.

* Less than 1 percent.

n.a. = Not available.

Table 7A: 75 Top Donors, Contributions as a Percent of U.S. and Worldwide Pretax Income, 1988

Company Rank	Contributions[1] (dollars)	U.S. Pretax Income[2] ($ Thousands)	Contributions as Percent of U.S. Pretax Income	Worldwide Pretax Income[2] ($ Thousands)	Contributions as Percent of Worldwide Pretax Income
1	$ 74,965,035	$ 1,945,000	3.9%	$ 9,033,000	0.8%
2	52,343,196	4,941,000	1.1	5,940,000	0.9
3	50,916,000	3,170,800	1.6	6,734,900	0.8
4	47,411,026	1,540,000	3.1	3,286,000	2.1
5	43,491,206	n.a.	n.a.	*	*
6	34,684,591	2,652,000	1.3	8,300,000	0.4
7	34,335,901	n.a.	n.a.	1,453,700	2.4
8	34,244,678	1,962,000	1.7	3,824,000	0.9
9	30,311,000	n.a.	n.a.	1,630,000	1.9
10	29,864,949	4,625,000	9.6	8,342,500	0.4
11	29,089,521	1,101,000	2.6	1,882,000	1.5
12	27,628,677	n.a.	n.a.	1,700,000	1.6
13	26,061,591	n.a.	n.a.	1,142,000	2.3
14	23,725,000	527,000	4.5	1,396,000	1.7
15	22,888,549	n.a.	n.a.	3,307,000	0.7
16	21,667,769	n.a.	n.a.	1,065,500	2.0
17	20,775,341	2,563,000	0.8	2,802,000	0.7
18	20,138,000	1,821,000	1.1	2,236,000	0.9
19	19,962,699	n.a.	n.a.	2,459,000	0.8
20	19,791,515	1,746,000	1.1	3,867,000	0.5
21	18,942,715	n.a.	n.a.	1,331,000	1.4
22	18,636,818	n.a.	n.a.	1,909,000	1.0
23	18,826,369	n.a.	n.a.	1,115,800	1.6
24	17,365,792	472,000	3.7	n.a.	n.a.
25	17,000,000	n.a.	n.a.	1,005,000	1.7
26	16,839,000	n.a.	n.a.	2,899,000	0.6
27	15,589,448	970,000	1.6	n.a.	n.a.
28	15,417,412	n.a.	n.a.	n.a.	n.a.
29	15,368,288	n.a.	n.a.	3,461,000	0.4
30	15,146,000	n.a.	n.a.	2,431,000	0.6
31	15,098,426	820,000	1.8	820,000	1.8
32	15,024,198	685,710	2.2	763,081	2.0
33	14,989,000	n.a.	n.a.	1,410,100	1.1
34	14,121,000	n.a.	n.a.	1,871,000	0.8
35	12,259,835	251,282	4.9	513,336	2.4
36	11,993,524	n.a.	n.a.	1,055,476	1.1
37	11,668,965	n.a.	n.a.	1,103,800	1.1
38	11,644,317	n.a.	n.a.	156,000	7.5
39	11,630,400	n.a.	n.a.	1,160,100	1.0
40	11,611,565	n.a.	n.a.	893,000	1.3
41	11,436,722	n.a.	n.a.	1,692,200	0.7
42	11,409,000	n.a.	n.a.	1,164,900	1.0
43	11,328,750	n.a.	n.a.	1,285,300	0.9
44	11,100,426	933,000	1.2	905,000	1.2
45	11,032,221	n.a.	n.a.	1,056,551	1.0
46	10,891,818	n.a.	n.a.	2,707,000	0.4
47	10,817,085	n.a.	n.a.	1,058,874	1.0
48	10,702,208	n.a.	n.a.	2,129,000	0.5
49	10,619,279	n.a.	n.a.	1,137,600	0.9
50	10,455,332	n.a.	n.a.	1,635,100	0.6

[1]Direct giving and company foundation pay-outs included; grants made to and retained by company foundations are excluded.

[2]Domestic and worldwide pretax income rounded, percentages actual.

*Company showed loss.

n.a. = Not available.

Table 7A: 75 Top Donors, Contributions as a Percent of U.S. and Worldwide Income, 1988 (continued)

Company Rank	Contributions[1] (dollars)	U.S. Pretax Income[2] ($ Thousands)	Contributions as Percent of U.S. Pretax Income	Worldwide Pretax Income[2] ($ Thousands)	Contributions as Percent of Worldwide Pretax Income
51	10,300,250	n.a.	n.a.	379,617	2.7
52	10,198,285	n.a.	n.a.	265,400	3.8
53	9,835,000	n.a.	n.a.	781,000	1.3
54	9,604,562	402,000	2.4	377,300	2.5
55	9,322,470	1,972,000	0.5	n.a.	n.a.
56	9,281,336	418,000	2.2	633,000	1.5
57	8,860,300	n.a.	n.a.	872,000	1.0
58	8,762,730	n.a.	n.a.	*	n.a.
59	8,573,754	n.a.	n.a.	2,389,000	0.4
60	8,330,599	n.a.	n.a.	508,100	1.6
61	8,222,587	n.a.	n.a.	507,000	1.6
62	8,158,855	n.a.	n.a.	420,000	1.9
63	8,039,734	n.a.	n.a.	1,014,200	0.8
64	7,747,772	416,700	1.9	497,600	1.6
65	7,411,618	n.a.	n.a.	1,314,500	0.6
66	7,220,000	687,400	1.1	958,600	0.8
67	6,862,143	*	n.a.	n.a.	n.a.
68	6,760,000	n.a.	n.a.	*	n.a.
69	6,630,000	n.a.	n.a.	907,900	0.7
70	6,290,881	n.a.	n.a.	308,400	2.0
71	5,984,000	n.a.	n.a.	n.a.	n.a.
72	5,716,275	n.a.	n.a.	842,000	0.7
73	5,662,829	n.a.	n.a.	270,600	2.1
74	5,598,940	n.a.	n.a.	612,717	0.9
75	5,326,587	n.a.	n.a.	271,001	2.0

[1]Direct giving and company foundation pay-outs included; grants made to and retained by company foundations are excluded.

[2]U.S. and worldwide pretax income rounded, percentages actual.

*Company showed loss.

n.a. = Not available.

Table 7B: 75 Top Donors, Corporate Social Expenditures as a Percent of U.S. and Worldwide Pretax Income, 1988

Company Rank	Total of Corporate Assistance and Contributions	Corporate Social Expenditure As a Percent of		Rank for Corporate Assistance Only	Rank for Cash Only
		U.S. Pretax Income	Worldwide Pretax Income		
1	$ 93,831,435	4.8	1.0	2	1
2	85,728,677	n.a.	5.0	1	23
3	60,458,996	1.2	1.0	5	2
4	39,010,168	1.5	0.5	8	3
5	32,655,269	3.0	1.7	9	15
6	27,693,411	n.a.	1.5	4	7
7	25,273,000	n.a.	2.2	3	16
8	25,108,000	4.8	1.8	19	11
9	23,876,549	n.a.	0.7	28	4
10	22,775,769	n.a.	2.1	24	13
11	21,942,715	n.a.	1.6	12	6
12	21,875,341	0.9	0.8	25	10
13	20,746,000	n.a.	1.1	6	22
14	20,302,000	n.a.	0.7	11	9
15	20,224,400	1.1	0.9	91	5
16	18,902,791	n.a.	1.7	36	28
17	18,300,000	n.a.	1.8	21	8
18	18,031,592	2.2	2.2	13	12
19	16,295,802	n.a.	n.a.	29	38
20	16,024,198	2.3	2.1	26	14
21	14,613,922	1.6	1.6	10	17
22	12,857,064	n.a.	1.2	17	19
23	12,659,835	5.0	2.5	42	21
24	12,312,736	n.a.	0.8	17	32
25	11,062,221	n.a.	1.0	119	18
26	10,619,281	n.a.	0.9	156	20
27	10,584,785	n.a.	4.0	44	27
28	10,041,612	0.5	n.a.	34	24
29	9,553,336	2.3	1.5	52	25
30	8,415,373	2.0	1.7	35	29
31	8,302,587	n.a.	1.6	43	26
32	7,534,329	n.a.	3.5	7	56
33	7,438,448	n.a.	n.a.	37	30
34	7,260,000	n.a.	n.a.	40	31
35	6,424,852	n.a.	1.2	18	50
36	6,322,601	n.a.	2.7	15	43
37	5,916,078	n.a.	2.2	55	33
38	5,633,527	n.a.	0.9	118	34
39	5,513,228	n.a.	0.5	47	35
40	5,457,243	n.a.	1.8	14	55
41	5,348,015	1.4	1.1	53	45
42	5,164,006	n.a.	n.a.	56	36
43	5,162,289	3.3	1.5	20	42
44	5,013,000	n.a.	2.3	57	66
45	5,002,500	2.2	n.a.	182	156
46	4,996,949	0.5	n.a.	41	155
47	4,906,595	n.a.	0.5	145	37
48	4,610,015	2.2	1.3	38	40
49	4,403,456	1.7	1.0	22	47
50	4,228,980	1.2	1.2	115	39

n.a. = Not available.

Table 7B: 75 Top Donors, Corporate Social Expenditures as a Percent of U.S. and Worldwide Pretax Income, 1988 (continued)

Company Rank	Total of Corporate Assistance and Contributions	Corporate Social Expenditure As a Percent of		Rank for Corporate Assistance Only	Rank for Cash Only
		U.S. Pretax Income	Worldwide Pretax Income		
51	4,113,049	n.a.	0.6	31	44
52	4,004,500	n.a.	0.3	77	41
53	3,974,873	2.1	n.a.	27	48
54	3,433,000	n.a.	1.1	96	64
55	3,362,359	0.7	0.4	83	46
56	3,189,913	0.7	0.5	43	51
57	3,097,870	1.5	n.a.	46	53
58	3,073,000	n.a.	0.5	86	49
59	3,000,000	n.a.	0.7	61	52
60	2,928,100	1.6	n.a.	49	54
61	2,797,120	n.a.	2.1	45	57
62	2,733,172	0.5	n.a.	33	65
63	2,703,983	0.6	0.5	63	63
64	2,413,600	0.7	n.a.	75	59
65	2,381,578	n.a.	n.a.	120	58
66	2,365,476	1.3	1.2	32	69
67	2,200,801	0.8	n.a.	87	60
68	2,168,000	n.a.	n.a.	94	61
69	2,154,423	2.1	n.a.	39	68
70	2,046,854	n.a.	1.0	78	62
71	1,973,397	n.a.	0.8	30	75
72	1,964,000	n.a.	n.a.	23	150
73	1,825,709	n.a.	0.5	79	67
74	1,750,219	1.8	n.a.	101	70
75	1,557,342	n.a.	n.a.	51	71

n.a. = Not available.

Table 8: Anticipated Changes in Contributions Budgets, 1988-1989
by Industry

Industry Classification	Number of Companies	1988-1989 Average Anticipated Percentage Change	1988-1989 Median Anticipated Percentage Change
Chemicals	16	8%	9%
Electrical machinery (except computers)	8	11	3
Food, beverage and tobacco	11	10	10
Industrial machinery and computers	16	14	10
Paper and like products	15	6	7
Petroleum and gas[1]	19	10	12
Pharmaceuticals	14	4	5
Other manufacturing[2]	30	4	7
Printing and publishing	6	− 6	− 2
Textiles and apparel	4	− 9	− 4
Transportation equipment[3]	20	8	6
Total: Manufacturing	159	7%	7%
Banking	39	8	6
Business services[4]	18	6	1
Finance	6	14	11
Insurance	38	6	5
Retail and wholesale trade	13	6	1
Telecommunications	12	6	5
Transportation	7	0	7
Utilities	43	7	3
Total: Nonmanufacturing	176	7%	4%
Total: All Companies	335	7%	6%

[1]Includes mining companies.
[2]Includes primary metals, fabricated metal products, and stone, clay and glass products.
[3]Includes tire manufacturers.
[4]Includes engineering and construction companies.

Table 9: Anticipated Changes in Contributions Budgets, 1988-89
By Program Size

Program Size	Number of Companies	Median Percentage Increase 1988-1989	Aggregate Percentage Increase 1988-1989
Less than $500,000	90	5.4%	4.7%
$500,000 to $999,999	66	8.6	5.5
$1 million to $499,999	103	4.7	4.2
$5 million and over	76	5.7	4.2
Total	335	5.6%	4.7%

Table 10: Corporate Assistance Expenditures, Summarized, 1988

Description	Number of Companies	Sum ($ Thousands)	Median
Cash Disbursements to 501(C) (3) Organizations Not Reported as Charitable Contributions	60	$ 80,395	$104,995
Loan of Company Personnel	54	13,333	41,048
Donations of Product and Property Not Reported as Charitable Contributions	45	56,183	30,960
Use of Corporate Facilities or Services	45	1,699	15,000
Administrative Cost for Contributions Function	104	28,802	81,989
Total	157	$180,400	$125,000

Table 11: Corporate Assistance Expenditures, by Industry 1988

Industry Classification	Number of Companies	Sums Total Corporate Assistance (000's)	Sums Corporate Assistance as Percent of Total Contributions	Medians Total Corporate Assistance	Medians Corporate Assistance as Percent of Total Contributions
Chemicals	6	$ 6,390	13%	$1,024,262	36%
Electrical machinery (except computers).....	4	595	14	11,500	8
Food, beverage and tobacco	7	11,005	39	212,547	7
Industrial machinery and computers	8	93,288	58	3,978,934	36
Paper and like products	6	5,081	13	318,293	13
Petroleum and gas[1]	12	11,563	11	267,500	7
Pharmaceuticals	8	9,362	13	256,000	6
Other manufacturing[2]	13	4,952	6	86,400	5
Printing and publishing...................	2	894	*	*	*
Textiles and apparel	2	54	*	*	*
Transportation equipment[3]	6	4,731	12	261,000	4
Total: Manufacturing	74	$151,605	18%	$ 231,274	7%
Banking	25	7,299	11	132,000	10
Business services[4]	6	2,372	35	210,966	15
Finance	4	3,265	9	117,500	5
Insurance.........................	18	6,433	16	49,202	7
Retail and wholesale trade................	2	322	*	*	*
Telecommunications	3	10,009	*	*	*
Transportation	3	235	*	*	*
Utilities..........................	22	2,465	15	59,130	12
Total: Nonmanufacturing	83	$ 32,400	17%	$ 100,000	10%
Total: All Companies...................	157	$184,005	18%	$ 125,000	9%

[1]Includes mining companies.
[2]Includes primary metal industries, fabricated metal products, and stone, clay and glass product.
[3]Includes tire manufacturers.
[4]Includes engineering and construction companies.
*Totals include all cases, but details omit industries with fewer than 4 cases.

Table 12: Program Administration Cost as a Percent of Contributions Budget
Medians by Size of Contributions Budget

Size of Contributions Budget	Number of Companies	Administrative Cost as a Percent of Contributions Budget (Median)
Under $500,000	25	5.7%
$500,000—$1 million	20	10.4
$1 million—$5 million	35	6.1
Over $5 million.............	25	5.2
Total	105	6.6%

Median Value of Administrative Costs: $83,500

Table 13: Foundations, by Industry
Companies Grouped by Industry Class

Industry Classification	Number of Companies	Number of Foundations	Percent of Companies with Foundations
Chemicals	16	10	63%
Electrical machinery (except computers)	10	8	80
Food, beverage and tobacco	12	11	91
Industrial machinery and computers	16	8	50
Paper and like products	15	12	80
Petroleum and gas[1]	21	11	52
Pharmaceuticals	17	13	77
Other manufacturing[2]	30	24	88
Printing and publishing	6	3	50
Textiles and apparel	4	1	25
Transportation equipment[3]	19	14	74
Total: Manufacturing	166	115	69%
Banking	40	26	65
Business services[4]	18	10	56
Finance	6	4	67
Insurance	36	24	67
Retail and wholesale trade	15	12	80
Telecommunications	12	8	67
Transportation	7	2	29
Utilities	47	10	21
Total: Nonmanufacturing	181	96	53%
Total: All Companies	347	211	61%

[1]Includes mining companies.
[2]Includes primary metal industries, fabricated metal products, and stone, clay and glass products.
[3]Includes tire manufacturers.
[4]Includes engineering and construction companies.

Table 14: Federated Campaigns, Median Contributions

Program Size	Number of Companies	Median Contribution to Federated Campaign
Less than $500,000	82	$ 61,954
$500,000 to $1 million	52	196,781
$1 million to $5 million	93	399,000
$5 million and over	73	1,724,130
Total	300	$ 283,282

Table 15: Giving by Regional Headquarters, 1988[a]

Region	Number of Companies	Total Contributions ($ millions)	Federated Campaigns	Health and Human Services		Education	Culture and Arts	Civic and Community	Other	Unspecified
				Other Health and Human Services	Total Health and Human Services					
New England............ (Maine, New Hampshire, Vermont, Massachusetts. Rhode Island, Connecticut)	36	$ 173.7	18%	11%	37%	32%	10%	15%	5%	0
Middle Atlantic:.......... (New York, New Jersey, Pennsylvania)	87	513.3	19	13	37	31	11	12	6	3%
East North Central:........ (Illinois, Ohio, Indiana, Michigan, Wisconsin)	81	386.2	21	11	38	30	10	15	5	2
West North Central: .... (Iowa, Kansas, Minnesota, Missouri, Nebraska, North Dakota, South Dakota)	23	103.9	18	17	36	30	14	14	5	1
South Atlantic:............ (Delaware, District of Columbia, Florida, Georgia, Maryland, North Carolina, South Carolina, Virginia, West Virginia Puerto Rico, Virgin Islands)	35	154.3	15	12	34	31	13	14	5	0
East South Central: .... (Alabama, Kentucky Mississippi, Tennessee)	16	26.8	16	7	30	31	13	22	4	0
West South Central: .... (Arkansas, Louisiana, Oklahoma, Texas)	18	53.9	18	10	34	29	13	15	2	7
Mountain: .... (Arizona, Colorado, Idaho, Montana, Nevada, New Mexico. Utah, Wyoming)	18	83.7	17	16	36	25	12	14	7	5
Pacific:................. (Alaska, California, Guam, Hawaii, Oregon, Washington)	42	149.4	24	13	42	30	10	10	5	4
Total	356	$1,645.2	19%	12%	37%	30%	11%	14%	5%	2%

[a]Total for a region may not add to 100 percent because of rounding.

Table 16: Sources of Corporate Contributions, 1984-1988
(millions of dollars)

	1988	1987	1986	1985	1984
Total company contributions	$1,376.4 (345)	$1,555.2 (315)	$1,688.6 (353)	$1,666.5 (423)	$1,448.9 (404)
Less: Grants to company foundations	433.6 (129)	486.8 (129)	649.1 (157)	614.0 (182)	562.2 (157)
Other company contributions	942.8 (327)	1,068.5 (293)	1,039.5 (334)	1,052.5 (395)	886.7 (388)
Plus: Contributions by company foundations . .	702.9 (204)	609.9 (196)	641.0 (224)	658.4 (256)	569.2 (230)
Total corporate contributions	$1,645.7 (356)	$1,678.3 (328)	$1,680.4 (372)	$1,710.9 (439)	$1,455.9 (422)

(Numbers in parentheses are responding companies).

Table 17: Foundations, Relationship Between Payouts and Pay-ins, 1984-1988
(millions of dollars)

Category	1988	1987	1986	1985	1984
Grants to company foundations	$433.6	$486.8	$649.1	$614.0	$562.2
Contributions by company foundations	702.9	609.9	641.0	658.4	569.2
Payouts less pay-ins	269.3	123.1	(8.1)	44.4	7.0
Percent payouts exceeded pay-ins	62.11%	25.29%	−1.25%	7.23%	1.25%

Table 18: Flow of Funds Into and Out of Foundations, 1984 to 1988

	1988		1987		1986		1985		1984	
	Number of Companies	Percent of Total	Number of Companies	Percent of Total	Number of Companies	Percent of Total	Number of Companies	Percent of Total	Number of Companies	Percent of Total
Pay-ins equal to payouts	11	9%	26	12%	22	9%	25	9%	16	7%
Pay-ins less than payouts	60	48	120	56	136	57	162	60	143	59
Pay-ins greater than payouts	53	43	67	32	82	34	82	30	84	34
Total	124	100%	213	100%	240	100%	269	100%	243	100%

Table 19: Contributions as a Percent of Pretax Income, Quartiles, 1979 to 1988[1]

	Contributions as a Percent of U.S. Income			Contributions as a Percent of Worldwide Income		
	Lower Quartile	Median	Upper Quartile	Lower Quartile	Median	Upper Quartile
1979	0.40%	0.69%	1.15%	0.36%	0.50%	1.00%
1980	0.40	0.73	1.34	0.37	0.66	1.16
1981	0.40	0.81	1.47	0.40	0.72	1.23
1982	0.54	1.13	1.85	0.53	0.99	1.62
1983	0.63	1.12	1.97	0.52	0.94	1.65
1984	0.56	1.03	1.88	0.53	0.85	1.54
1985	0.63	1.18	2.04	0.58	0.99	1.60
1986	0.66	1.17	2.10	0.59	1.01	1.63
1987	0.56	1.05	2.03	0.50	0.85	1.64
1988	0.52	0.87	1.58	0.51	0.83	1.30

[1]In each table using medians or quartiles, the data for each group (e.g., an industry class, an asset or income-size group) are placed in rank order from the lowest to the highest value, and divided into quarters. The first quartile is 25 percent of the way from the bottom number in the ranking; the median is the middle value in the ranking; and the third quartile is then 75 percent of the way between the lowest and the highest value. The "total" line on each table provides the quartiles (or median) for all of the companies included in that table.

Table 20A: Contributions as a Percent of U.S. Pretax Income, Quartiles, 1988
Companies Grouped by Dollar Size of Program

Program Size	Number of Companies	Lower Quartile	Median	Upper Quartile
Under $500,000	53	0.3%	0.8%	1.1%
$500,000 to $1 million	36	0.5	0.0	1.4
$1 million to $5 million	51	0.6	0.8	1.6
$5 million and over	24	1.1	1.7	2.5
All Groups	164	0.5	0.9	1.6

Table 20B: Contributions as a Percent of Worldwide Pretax Income, Quartiles, 1988
Companies Grouped by Dollar Size of Program

Program Size	Number of Companies	Lower Quartile	Median	Upper Quartile
Under $500,000	32	0.5%	0.6%	1.1%
$500,000 to $1 million	35	0.3	0.6	1.5
$1 million to $5 million	60	0.5	0.8	1.1
$5 million and over	72	0.7	1.0	1.7
All Groups	199	0.5	0.8	1.3

Table 21A: Contributions as a Percent of U.S. Pretax Income—Quartiles, 1988
Companies Grouped by Size of U.S. Income

U.S. Pretax Income	Number of Companies	Contributions Ratios[1]		
		Lower Quartile	Median	Upper Quartile[2]
Below $5 million	2	2.5	2.5	2.5
$5-9.9 million	8	1.6	4.2	13.4
$10-24.9 million	10	0.9	1.3	2.4
$25-49.9 million	31	0.8	1.1	1.8
$50-99.9 million	19	0.5	0.6	1.3
$100-249.9 million	38	0.4	0.7	1.1
$250-499.9 million	28	0.4	0.7	1.2
$500-999.9 million	15	0.3	0.5	1.6
$1 billion and over	15	0.5	1.1	1.7
All Income Groups	**166**	**0.5**	**0.9**	**1.6**

[1]The statistics presented here are derived only from companies with positive income.
[2]This is the 75th percentile.

Table 21B: Contributions as a Percent of Worldwide Pretax Income—Quartiles, 1988
Companies Grouped by Size of Worldwide Income

Worldwide Pretax Income	Number of Companies	Contributions Ratios[1]		
		Lower Quartile	Median	Upper Quartile[2]
Below $5 million	2	3.2	11.7	20.2
$5-9.9 million	2	2.7	3.6	4.6
$10-24.9 million	11	0.7	1.2	2.4
$25-49.9 million	14	0.7	1.1	1.6
$50-99.9 million	23	0.5	0.6	1.2
$100-249.9 million	32	0.5	0.8	1.1
$250-499.9 million	29	0.4	0.8	1.6
$500-999.9 million	38	0.5	0.7	1.0
$1 billion and over	48	0.5	0.9	1.1
All Income Groups	**199**	**0.5**	**0.8**	**1.3**

[1]The statistics presented here are derived only from companies with positive income.
[2]This is the 75th percentile.

Table 22A: Contributions as a Percent of U.S. Pretax Income—Quartiles, 1988
Companies Grouped by Industry Class

Industrial Classification	Number of Companies	Contributions Ratios[1]		
		Lower Quartile	Median	Upper Quartile[2]
Chemicals	7	1.1%	1.7%	2.4%
Electrical machinery (except computers).	5	0.5	1.2	1.9
Food, beverage and tobacco	*	*	*	*
Industrial machinery and computers	6	1.1	1.4	2.6
Paper and like products	8	0.6	0.7	1.1
Petroleum and gas[3]	4	0.5	0.7	1.1
Pharmaceuticals	4	1.1	2.3	3.9
Other manufacturing[4]	8	0.8	1.1	1.7
Printing and publishing	*	*	*	*
Textiles and apparel	*	*	*	*
Transportation equipment[5]	6	0.9	1.7	2.2
Banking	22	0.7	1.2	1.9
Business services[6]	4	0.3	0.5	0.9
Finance	*	*	*	*
Insurance	29	0.6	1.2	2.2
Retail and wholesale trade	7	1.3	1.6	3.7
Telecommunications	6	0.5	0.6	0.7
Transportation	*	*	*	*
Utilities	40	0.3	0.5	0.8

[1]The statistics presented here are derived only from companies with positive income.
[2]This is the 75th percentile.
[3]Includes mining companies.
[4]Includes primary metal industries, fabricated metal products, and stone, clay and glass products.
[5]Includes tire manufacturers.
[6]Includes engineering and construction companies.
*Fewer than 4 companies reporting.

Table 22B: Contributions as a Percent of Worldwide Pretax Income—Quartiles, 1988
Companies Grouped by Industry Class

Industrial Classification	Number of Companies	Contributions Ratios[1]		
		Lower Quartile	Median	Upper Quartile[2]
Chemicals	16	0.4%	0.7%	0.9%
Electrical machinery (except computers)	8	0.5	0.6	0.7
Food, beverage and tobacco	10	0.8	1.0	1.5
Industrial machinery and computers	15	0.7	0.9	1.5
Paper and like products	12	0.3	0.6	0.8
Petroleum and gas[3]	18	0.4	0.5	0.8
Pharmaceuticals	14	1.0	1.1	1.8
Other manufacturing[4]	24	0.5	0.8	1.8
Printing and publishing	4	1.5	2.3	2.6
Textiles and apparel	*	*	*	*
Transportation equipment[5]	14	0.8	1.1	1.6
Banking	13	0.5	0.7	1.0
Business services[6]	10	0.5	0.9	1.4
Finance	5	0.5	0.7	1.0
Insurance	13	0.6	1.2	2.0
Retail and wholesale trade	8	0.7	1.2	2.2
Telecommunications	5	0.6	0.7	1.0
Transportation	*	*	*	*
Utilities	6	0.3	0.4	0.9

[1]The statistics presented here are derived only from companies with positive income.
[2]This is the 75th percentile.
[3]Includes mining companies.
[4]Includes primary metal industries, fabricated metal products, and stone, clay and glass products.
[5]Includes tire manufacturers.
[6]Includes engineering and construction companies.
*Fewer than 4 companies reporting.

Table 23A: Contributions as a Percent of U.S. Pretax Income—Quartiles, 1988
Companies Grouped by Size of U.S. Assets

Assets	Number of Companies	Contributions' Ratios[1]		
		Lower Quartile	Median	Upper Quartile[2]
Below $100 million	13	1.2	1.9	4.9
$100-199 million	3	*	*	
$200-299 million	5	0.8	0.8	1.1
$300-499 million	8	0.9	1.2	1.4
$500-999 million	18	0.5	0.8	1.1
$1-1.9 billion	23	0.2	0.5	1.2
$2-2.9 billion	11	0.6	0.9	1.3
$3-3.9 billion	10	0.6	1.0	2.0
$4-4.9 billion	12	0.4	1.0	2.4
$5-9.9 billion	28	0.4	0.7	1.3
$10 billion and over	33	0.5	0.8	1.6
All Asset Groups	**164**	**0.5**	**0.9**	**1.6**

[1]The statistics presented here are derived only from companies with positive income.
[2]This is the 75th percentile.
*Categories with fewer than 4 cases are excluded.

Table 23B: Contributions as a Percent of Worldwide Pretax Income—Quartiles, 1988
Companies Grouped by Size of Worldwide Assets

Assets	Number of Companies	Contributions' Ratios[1]		
		Lower Quartile	Median	Upper Quartile[2]
Below $100 million	2	*	*	*
$100-199 million	5	0.7%	1.2%	2.4%
$200-299 million	6	0.5	1.3	3.2
$300-499 million	17	0.5	0.8	1.2
$500-999 million	18	0.5	1.0	1.5
$1-1.9 billion	27	0.3	0.8	1.1
$2-2.9 billion	15	0.5	0.8	2.1
$3-3.9 billion	12	0.5	0.9	1.2
$4-4.9 billion	10	0.5	0.8	1.9
$5-9.9 billion	33	0.6	1.0	1.9
$10 billion and over	54	0.5	0.8	1.2
All Asset Groups	**199**	**0.5**	**0.8**	**1.3**

[1]The statistics presented here are derived only from companies with positive income.
[2]This is the 75th percentile.
*Categories with fewer than 4 cases are excluded.

Table 24A: Contributions as a Percent of U.S. Pretax Income, Quartiles, 1988
Companies Grouped by Size of U.S. Sales

U.S. Sales	Number of Companies	Lower Quartile	Median	Upper Quartile
Below $250 million	16	1.0	1.8	3.0
$250-$500 million	25	0.5	0.8	1.2
$500 million-$1 billion	31	0.4	0.8	1.5
$1 billion-$2.5 billion	34	0.4	0.8	1.3
$2.5 billion-$5 billion	23	0.3	0.7	1.3
$5 billion and over	30	0.5	1.1	1.7
Total	159	0.5	0.9	1.6

Table 24B: Contributions as a Percent of Worldwide Pretax Income, Quartiles, 1988
Companies Grouped by Size of Worldwide Sales

Worldwide Sales	Number of Companies	Lower Quartile[2]	Median	Upper Quartile
Below $250 million	7	0.7	1.0	2.7
$250-$500 million	18	0.5	0.6	1.9
$500 million-$1 billion	26	0.5	1.2	1.5
$1 billion-$2.5 billion	34	0.5	0.9	1.1
$2.5 billion-$5 billion	33	0.3	0.7	1.1
$5 billion and over	81	0.6	0.8	1.5
Total	199	0.5	0.8	1.3

Table 25: Beneficiaries of Company Support, Quartiles, 1988
  Companies Grouped by Dollar Size of Program

Program Size	Number of Companies	Health and Human Services			Education			Culture and Art		
		Lower Quartile	Median	Upper Quartile	Lower Quartile	Median	Upper Quartile	Lower Quartile	Median	Upper Quartile
Less than $500,000	98	31.2%	44.5%	54.6%	15.8%	21.9%	25.0%	4.8%	7.6%	14.3%
$500,000 to $1 million	69	37.1	41.1	52.5	13.3	23.1	33.4	4.6	9.0	16.4
$1 million to $5 million	106	27.8	37.2	46.9	21.7	28.8	42.2	4.8	10.5	16.7
$5 million and over	81	20.0	27.0	35.7	26.2	32.8	46.6	5.8	11.1	16.0
All Groups	354	25.4	36.7	49.3	18.3	27.3	40.7	4.9	9.6	15.6

Table 25: Beneficiaries of Company Support, Quartiles, 1988 (continued)

Program Size	Number of Companies	Civic and Community			Other		
		Lower Quartile	Median	Upper Quartile	Lower Quartile	Median	Upper Quartile
Less than $500,000	98	5.4%	11.1%	19.4%	0.0%	0.3%	6.4%
$500,000 to $1 million	69	8.8	15.2	23.5	0.0	1.5	6.1
$1 million to $5 million	106	5.6	10.4	15.1	0.0	1.1	4.2
$5 million and over	81	6.4	10.5	16.2	0.5	2.3	7.9
All Companies	354	6.3	11.3	17.7	0.0	1.2	6.2

Table 26: Beneficiaries of Company Support, 1988—Quartiles for Companies by Industry Class[1]

Industry Category	Number of Companies	Health and Human Services			Education		
		Lower Quartile	Median	Upper Quartile	Lower Quartile	Median	Upper Quartile
Chemicals	16	24.9%	30.0%	37.1%	36.5%	42.3%	46.3%
Electrical machinery (except computers)	9	37.3	43.2	50.5	35.3	37.5	40.0
Industrial machinery and computers	12	22.2	41.1	56.0	21.3	25.3	31.2
Food, beverage and tobacco	16	17.0	33.8	46.7	16.7	34.3	53.9
Paper and like products	12	23.2	32.7	40.0	26.5	29.3	48.8
Petroleum and gas[2]	22	20.6	27.6	38.3	29.1	44.1	57.3
Pharmaceuticals	16	16.2	24.9	46.7	15.0	24.2	38.2
Other manufacturing[3]	28	24.7	34.3	45.7	26.2	34.1	46.3
Printing and publishing	5	6.9	12.4	31.8	18.2	18.2	45.6
Textiles and apparel	4	7.8	16.0	24.4	37.5	51.6	64.5
Transportation equipment[4]	19	23.3	28.8	40.1	27.0	38.6	50.9
Total: Manufacturing	159	20.6	30.1	43.9	25.3	35.5	47.9
Banking	40	30.1	38.3	47.2	15.5	20.4	25.5
Business services[5]	15	27.1	33.7	50.8	10.3	23.3	33.5
Finance	6	38.0	42.0	55.2	21.7	28.6	29.8
Insurance	38	31.2	35.9	52.6	18.0	28.2	34.3
Retail and wholesale trade	15	35.1	52.3	60.6	13.3	20.2	30.4
Telecommunications	12	23.3	31.7	35.5	24.8	30.8	42.8
Transportation	6	31.0	39.3	47.3	13.4	26.9	35.6
Utilities	45	41.9	47.3	54.1	18.1	22.2	26.1
Total: Nonmanufacturing	177	31.1	42.3	52.5	17.3	22.2	30.6
Total: All Companies	336	25.9	36.7	49.0	18.9	27.6	40.7

[1]For an explanation of quartiles, see Table 19.
[2]Includes mining companies.
[3]Includes primary metal industries, fabricated metal products, and stone, clay and glass products.
[4]Includes tire manufacturers.
[5]Includes engineering and construction companies.

Table 26: Beneficiaries of Company Support, 1988 (continued)

Culture and Art			Civic and Community			Other		
Lower Quartile	Median	Upper Quartile	Lower Quartile	Median	Upper Quartile	Lower Quartile	Median	Upper Quartile
5.7%	8.8%	11.1%	9.1%	12.6%	15.3%	0.5%	3.1%	7.6%
5.3	11.8	12.5	2.3	7.1	9.7	1.2	1.5	3.0
4.0	7.5	10.8	5.2	11.7	15.6	1.0	4.3	7.3
4.3	8.8	12.3	4.6	8.6	20.1	1.3	3.4	9.4
2.0	5.2	12.0	9.1	12.1	19.2	1.6	3.2	11.0
6.4	9.6	13.4	7.7	14.8	17.8	0.7	2.9	7.4
1.9	4.9	8.8	7.1	10.9	16.4	2.0	5.3	36.9
4.0	8.5	15.9	8.1	11.8	16.1	0.8	1.8	3.8
5.6	13.1	20.8	6.2	8.9	12.9	1.5	5.7	23.9
0.7	1.3	4.7	10.2	19.4	25.0	7.9	15.1	17.5
5.3	10.8	14.3	5.9	9.6	19.6	1.4	3.0	6.6
4.2	8.6	12.9	6.8	11.1	16.6	1.1	2.8	8.0
11.1	15.6	19.7	11.5	15.7	20.0	1.8	4.7	9.8
2.8	9.5	20.0	8.3	12.4	18.0	5.2	7.0	29.6
7.5	10.5	17.0	8.2	8.4	9.0	0.2	0.7	1.3
6.0	11.5	16.6	8.1	14.9	20.0	0.5	2.1	5.3
5.7	9.7	18.3	6.9	14.8	20.8	1.1	3.4	7.2
14.4	17.7	23.2	5.2	8.2	15.5	0.6	3.6	8.0
6.0	13.0	19.1	3.5	11.0	18.9	0.2	4.0	7.4
6.0	9.1	13.6	5.4	11.4	21.6	1.1	3.0	8.6
6.8	11.9	17.9	7.3	13.4	19.8	0.9	3.6	8.6
5.2	9.8	15.7	7.0	11.9	17.8	1.1	3.3	8.4

Table 27A: Contributions as a Percent of U.S. Pretax Income, 1988
Grouped by Rate of Giving

Contributions as Percent of Pretax Income	U.S. Pretax Income					
	All Companies	Manufacturing	Banking	Insurance[1]	Utilities and Telecommunication	Other Service
	(Number of Companies)[2]					
0- .24%	20	1	1	4	9	4
.25- .49	22	2	1	3	14	2
.50- .74	27	8	4	2	11	2
.75- .99	21	8	4	3	5	1
1.0-1.49	33	13	5	6	5	4
1.5-1.99	16	6	5	3	1	1
2.0-2.99	13	6	3	3	1	0
3.0-3.99	6	2	0	2	0	2
4.0-4.99	4	3	0	1	0	0
5.0 and over	4	1	0	2	0	1
Total	166	51	23	29	46	17

Table 27B: Contributions as a Percent of Worldwide Pretax Income, 1988
Grouped by Rate of Giving

Contributions as Percent of Pretax Income	All Companies	Manufacturing	Banking	Insurance[1]	Utilities and Telecommunication	Other Service
	(Number of Companies)[2]					
0- .24%	15	12	0	1	2	0
.25- .49	32	20	2	2	3	5
.50- .74	41	28	5	1	2	5
.75- .99	32	23	2	1	3	3
1.0-1.49	38	25	2	3	1	7
1.5-1.99	19	14	2	2	0	1
2.0-2.99	15	11	0	1	0	3
3.0-3.99	2	2	0	0	0	0
4.0-4.99	2	1	0	1	0	0
5.0 and over	4	2	0	1	0	1
Total	200	138	13	13	11	25

[1]Insurance company figures are based on "net gain from operations after dividends to policyholders and before federal income tax, excluding capital gains and losses"—the closest measure to pretax income of corporations generally.
[2]Loss companies excluded.

Method Tables

Table 28: Participants by Size of Contributions Program, 1986 to 1988

| | 1988 | | 1987 | | 1986 | |
Program Size	Number	Percent	Number	Percent	Number	Percent
Less than $500,000	98	28%	74	23%	87	23%
$500,000 to $1 million	69	19	62	19	72	19
$1 million to $5 million	108	30	111	34	128	35
$5 million and over	81	23	81	25	85	23
Total	356	100%	328	100%	372	100%

Totals may not add to 100 percent due to rounding.

Table 29: Participants by Worldwide Sales, 1988

| | Manufacturing Companies | | Selected Nonmanufacturing Companies[1] | |
Worldwide Sales	Number	Percent	Number	Percent
Below $250 million	7	5%	2	3%
$250-500 million	14	9	5	8
$500 million-1 billion	14	9	12	18
$1 billion-2.5 billion	35	23	10	15
$2.5 billion-5 billion	24	16	9	14
$5 billion and over	57	38	28	42
Total	151	100%	66	100%

[1]Banking, insurance, telecommunications and utilities are excluded from nonmanufacturing companies and reported in Table 30.

Table 30: Participants by Worldwide Assets, 1988: Banking, Insurance, Telephone, Gas and Electric Utilities

Worldwide Assets	Banking		Insurance		Telecommunications		Utilities	
	Number	Percent	Number	Percent	Number	Percent	Number	Percent
Under $250 million	—	—	—	—	—	—	1	14
$250-$500 million	—	—	1	8	—		—	—
$500 million-1 billion	—	—	1	0	—	—	—	—
$1 billion-2.5 billion	—		I	8	—	—	4	58
$2.5 billion-5 billion	1	7	1	8	—	—	1	14
$5 billion-10 billion	2	14	3	23	1	17	1	14
$10 billion and over	11	79	6	45	5	83	—	—
Total	14	100%	13	100%	6	100%	7	100%

Table 31: Manufacturing Participants in the Fortune 500 (Based on Total Worldwide Sales)

Rank	Number of Survey Respondents
Number 1- 100	55
101- 200	39
201- 300	14
301- 400	12
401- 500	12
Total	132

Table 32: Nonmanufacturing Participants in the Fortune Service 500

Industry Class (Top 500)	Number of Survey Respondents
Top 100 diversified service companies (ranked by sales)	10
Top 100 commercial banking companies (ranked by assets)	23
Top 50 savings institutions (ranked by assets)	1
Top 50 life insurance companies (ranked by assets)	13
Top 50 diversified financial companies (ranked by assets)	12
Top 50 retailing companies (ranked by sales)	3
Top 50 transportation companies (ranked by operating revenues)	5
Top 50 utilities (ranked by assets)	18
Total	85

Canadian Tables

Canadian Table 1: Canadian Donations as a Percentage of Pretax Income, 1988—Companies Grouped by Industry Class[1] (in Canadian dollars)

Industrial Classification	Number of Companies	Pretax Income (Thousands)	Contributions (Sum)	Pretax Income (Median) (Thousands)	Contributions (Median)	Contributions as % of Pretax Income (Median)
Chemicals	6	$ 403,402	$ 1,987,625	$ 57,310	$ 154,403	0.34
Electrical machinery (except computers)	2	312,948	2,091,993	156,474	1,045,997	0.58
Fabricated metal products	2	46,205	394,635	23,102	197,318	0.90
Food, beverage and tobacco	5	439,466	7,149,192	61,205	743,500	1.21
Industrial machinery and computers	5	717,390	3,778,575	37,070	119,675	0.32
Paper and like products[2]	9	2,284,659	8,355,845	215,782	478,403	0.39
Petroleum and gas[3]	6	3,122,797	13,682,925	288,925	1,317,401	0.42
Primary metal industries[4]	7	2,809,337	5,436,715	332,800	462,000	0.17
Printing and publishing	2	268,290	4,438,734	134,145	2,219,367	1.90
Stone, clay & glass	6	116,315	444,892	58,157	222,448	0.36
Textiles.	2	85,716	362,000	42,858	181,000	0.29
Transportation equipment[5]	4	267,546	1,055,822	66,230	226,411	0.38
Total: Manufacturing	52	10,874,071	49,178,613	71,625	391,839	0.40
Banking	2	1,182,393	4,195,050	591,196	2,097,525	0.39
Business services[6]	2	39,581	143,169	19,791	71,585	0.34
Finance	7	659,241	2,885,639	97,300	322,391	0.63
Retail and wholesale trade[7]	8	274,215	1,858,554	12,891	70,837	0.68
Telecommunications	9	3,503,740	7,989,076	78,200	480,000	0.23
Transportation	3	155,480	488,000	16,292	53,000	0.33
Utilities.	6	1,448,290	2,656,875	161,774	259,000	0.26
Holding companies	7	392,461	3,255,515	60,666	179,675	1.01
Total: Nonmanufacturing	44	7,655,401	23,471,878	56,450	229,000	0.43
Total: All Companies	96	$18,529,472	$72,650,491	$ 66,959	$ 322,454	0.41

[1]Loss companies excluded, which reduces total contributions in this table.
[2]Includes lumber and wood.
[3]Includes oil and gas extraction and refining.
[4]Includes mining and quarrying.
[5]Includes air, railroad and water transport.
[6]Includes engineering and construction companies.
[7]Includes durable and non-durable wholesale trade.

Canadian Table 2: Canadian Donations to Health and Human Services, 1988—Quartiles
Companies Grouped by Industry (in Canadian Dollars)

Industrial classification	Number of companies	Sum	Lower quartile	Median	Upper quartile
Chemicals	6	1,104,430	26,768	101,438	319,432
Electrical machinery (except computers)	3	951,033	27,000	50,133	873,900
Fabricated materials	2	177,070	40,000	88,555	137,070
Food, beverage and tobacco	8	3,320,148	36,414	69,896	388,150
Machinery and computers	5	1,732,980	28,603	90,125	792,825
Paper	9	2,623,312	105,250	265,600	480,522
Petroleum and gas	7	5,518,787	199,000	405,093	1,110,511
Pharmaceuticals	—	—	—	—	—
Primary metals	9	2,056,428	20,930	117,993	388,400
Printing and publishing	2	943,081	140,180	471,541	802,901
Stone, clay and glass	2	248,637	68,750	124,319	179,887
Textiles and apparel	2	156,500	2,500	78,250	154,000
Transportation equipment	4	583,376	53,939	149,503	234,091
Total: Manufacturing	59	18,424,780	42,905	140,180	394,700
Banking	2	2,419,475	911,000	1,209,738	1,508,475
Business services	4	92,724	7,825	17,250	44,688
Insurance	7	1,614,530	108,500	192,032	421,000
Retail and wholesale trade	11	960,103	15,000	42,998	93,389
Telecommunications	10	4,205,500	35,475	129,700	574,293
Transportation	4	276,000	15,750	20,500	170,750
Utilities	7	1,108,817	44,553	78,625	200,840
Holding companies	7	1,584,270	41,250	55,575	639,215
Total: Non-Manufacturing	52	12,262,419	24,700	73,188	218,000
Total: All Companies	111	30,687,199	35,000	105,000	349,880

Canadian Table 3: Canadian Donations to Education, 1988—Quartiles
Companies Grouped by Industry (in Canadian Dollars)

Industrial classification	Number of companies	Sum	Lower quartile	Median	Upper quartile
Chemicals	6	522,420	7,075	33,180	188,250
Electrical machinery (except computers)	3	407,583	25,000	58,250	324,313
Fabricated materials	2	100,800	33,800	50,400	67,000
Food, beverage and tobacco	8	1,387,310	25,913	97,453	227,583
Machinery and computers	5	1,547,660	10,650	19,660	753,350
Paper	9	3,304,741	66,658	111,100	745,388
Petroleum and gas	7	3,828,096	103,500	232,956	689,228
Pharmaceuticals	—	—	—	—	—
Primary metals	9	2,138,125	16,110	117,880	554,510
Printing and publishing	2	450,813	73,750	225,407	377,063
Stone, clay and glass	2	136,700	47,150	68,350	89,550
Textiles and apparel	2	89,500	2,000	44,750	87,500
Transportation equipment	4	280,570	16,688	45,600	148,140
Total: Manufacturing	59	14,194,298	25,000	89,550	291,000
Banking	2	913,052	335,000	456,526	578,052
Business services	3	27,745	2,700	5,100	19,945
Insurance	7	798,046	48,000	86,168	139,953
Retail and wholesale trade	11	544,868	3,750	17,165	50,000
Telecommunications	10	2,039,071	14,625	43,750	290,043
Transportation	3	129,000	10,000	12,000	107,000
Utilities	7	620,656	6,300	45,000	111,020
Holding companies	6	1,137,350	35,250	65,050	419,938
Total: Non-Manufacturing	49	6,209,788	11,000	42,100	159,027
Total: All Companies	108	20,404,086	17,374	72,500	203,500

Canadian Table 4: Canadian Donations to Culture and Art, 1988—Quartiles
Companies Grouped by Industry (in Canadian Dollars)

Industrial classification	Number of companies	Sum	Lower quartile	Median	Upper quartile
Chemicals	8	173,940	2,750	9,125	54,818
Electrical machinery (except computers)	3	671,080	800	3,000	667,000
Fabricated materials	1	31,035	—	—	—
Food, beverage and tobacco	8	977,070	6,154	42,625	113,425
Machinery and computers	4	236,800	1,625	2,650	173,325
Paper	9	994,146	25,900	110,047	182,995
Petroleum and gas	7	2,630,030	107,605	127,203	596,462
Primary metals	9	560,094	2,625	14,600	140,340
Printing and publishing	2	543,831	76,590	271,916	467,241
Stone, clay and glass	2	40,280	1,500	20,140	38,780
Textiles and apparel	1	52,500	—	—	—
Transportation equipment	4	82,530	8,100	12,250	43,548
Total: Manufacturing	56	6,993,621	5,475	36,535	123,888
Banking	2	326,065	143,065	164,033	185,000
Business services	2	74,500	27,500	37,250	47,000
Insurance	7	230,330	21,600	24,000	37,530
Retail and wholesale trade	9	165,190	3,233	5,800	27,750
Telecommunications	10	880,227	11,900	71,158	151,653
Transportation	3	56,000	6,000	20,000	30,000
Utilities	7	572,205	19,600	28,650	55,000
Holding companies	6	243,560	9,890	31,800	73,338
Total: Non-Manufacturing	46	2,550,077	7,228	28,075	70,204
Total: All Companies	102	9,543,698	7,228	30,000	106,401

Canadian Table 5: Canadian Donations to Civic and Community, 1988—Quartiles
Companies Grouped by Industry (in Canadian Dollars)

Industrial classification	Number of companies	Sum	Lower quartile	Median	Upper quartile
Chemicals	6	160,700	1,975	12,100	42,100
Electrical machinery (except computers)	3	116,317	4,000	5,817	106,500
Fabricated materials	1	441,650	—	—	—
Food, beverage and tobacco	8	3,061,143	14,029	36,500	126,316
Machinery and computers	4	242,285	4,601	26,775	150,338
Paper	9	903,888	26,035	69,500	182,384
Petroleum and gas	7	2,068,760	64,249	115,818	237,743
Primary metals	9	883,996	7,663	44,400	107,686
Printing and publishing	1	145,529	—	—	—
Stone, clay and glass	2	15,700	1,400	7,850	14,300
Textiles and apparel	2	32,000	7,500	16,000	24,500
Transportation equipment	3	75,311	3,050	22,861	49,400
Total: Manufacturing	55	7,947,279	12,000	42,000	115,331
Banking	2	344,322	168,322	172,161	176,000
Business services	3	47,600	800	2,000	44,800
Insurance	7	212,900	12,000	22,591	59,500
Retail and wholesale trade	10	356,610	2,050	6,725	44,639
Telecommunications	10	581,386	9,950	16,475	132,234
Transportation	3	62,000	14,000	20,000	28,000
Utilities	7	227,498	3,650	29,660	50,000
Holding companies	5	165,275	2,850	10,650	74,463
Total: Non-Manufacturing	47	1,997,591	5,000	17,105	50,000
Total: All Companies	102	9,944,870	6,950	23,881	98,965

Canadian Table 6: Canadian Donations to Other, 1988—Quartiles
Companies Grouped by Industry (in Canadian Dollars)

Industrial classification	Number of companies	Sum	Lower quartile	Median	Upper quartile
Chemicals	5	26,135	1,838	3,000	9,730
Electrical machinery (except computers)	2	6,000	1,000	3,000	5,000
Fabricated materials	1	44,180	—	—	—
Food, beverage and tobacco	7	289,134	1,360	10,000	72,850
Machinery and computers	2	11,300	1,000	5,650	10,300
Paper	6	529,758	37,614	61,310	158,563
Petroleum and gas	4	500,745	38,892	88,816	247,852
Primary metals	4	201,272	9,476	22,905	118,572
Printing and publishing	2	316,834	70,165	158,417	246,669
Stone, clay and glass	1	3,575	—	—	—
Textiles and apparel	1	31,500	—	—	—
Transportation equipment	2	34,035	10,535	17,018	23,500
Total: Manufacturing	37	1,994,468	4,288	31,500	71,508
Banking	2	190,136	58,000	95,068	132,136
Business services	—	—	—	—	—
Insurance	2	29,833	450	14,917	29,383
Retail and wholesale trade	4	77,895	2,151	10,343	45,928
Telecommunications	9	505,928	15,275	37,000	71,335
Transportation	2	27,000	2,000	13,500	25,000
Utilities	4	139,699	5,399	34,299	65,077
Holding companies	3	63,625	5,000	17,700	40,925
Total: Non-Manufacturing	26	1,034,116	4,619	24,434	51,375
Total: All Companies	63	3,028,584	5,000	25,000	58,000

Canadian Table 7: Distribution of Contributions (in Canadian Dollars)

	Number of Companies	Total (dollars)	Median
Health & Human Services	111	$30,687,199	$105,000
Federated giving	103	11,618,280	50,000
Hospitals	98	9,838,142	29,490
Matching gifts	20	411,380	10,000
All other	92	7,478,947	26,575
Unspecified		1,340,449	
Education	108	20,404,086	72,500
Higher education	90	13,365,932	50,000
Preschool	35	424,723	4,063
Scholarship	42	2,588,710	17,750
Education related	62	2,033,804	10,800
Matching gifts	19	799,353	8,000
Unspecified		1,191,564	
Culture and Arts	102	9,543,698	30,000
Matching gifts	9	54,952	4,465
All other culture and the arts	85	7,782,439	29,000
Unspecified		1,706,307	
Civic and Community	102	9,944,870	23,681
Public policy organizations	28	454,945	8,000
Community improvement	49	4,111,106	13,900
Environment & ecology	48	653,290	3,000
Justice & law	11	47,880	1,645
Housing	7	27,810	2,000
Other	70	2,993,816	9,795
Unspecified		1,656,024	
Total, Other	64	3,036,469	24,434
Unspecified Beneficiaries		1,508,595	
Total All Contributions	111	$75,124,917	$275,300

Canadian Table 8: Form of Contributions (in Canadian Dollars)

	Number of Companies	Total Value (Dollars)	Median
Total Contributions	111	$75,124,917	$275,300
Form			
Cash...	105	64,425,916	218,000
Gifts of securities	—	—	—
Gifts of company product ....,,,	14	3,592,167	20,000
Gifts of property other than company product	5	446,675	35,000
Unspecified	—	6,660,159	—

Total Contributions In Education	Number of Companies	Total Value (Dollars)	Median
Cash...	89	$15,312,303	$ 72,000
Gifts of securities	—	—	—
Gifts of company product	3	1,174,705	25,000
Gifts of property other than company product	1	275,000	275,000
Unspecified	—	3,632,078	—
Total	108	20,394,086	72,500

Canadian Table 9: Form of Corporate Assistance Expenditures (in Canadian Dollars)

	Number of Companies	Total Value (Dollars)	Median
Cash..	16	$4,811,860	$28,725
Loaned personal	18	372,323	13,500
Donated products	12	1,725,278	21,000
Facilities..	10	76,975	5,000
Administration	25	909,374	30,000
Total	33	$7,895,810	—

Canadian Table 10: Contributions for 15 Largest Donors—1988 (in Canadian Dollars)

	Total	Percentage of Pretax Income	Education
1	$7,666,000	0.44	$2,169,000
2	5,438,000	2.00	727,000
3	3,039,000	0.63	1,404,000
4	3,005,863	0.22	563,173
5	3,700,500	0.19	978,048
6	2,757,845	0.65	689,228
7	2,530,050	0.30	578,052
8	2,399,331	1.28	73,750
9	2,039,403	2.54	377,063
10	2,039,275	0.27	496,057
11	1,971,993	0.69	324,313
12	1,883,145	0.39	911,755
13	1,822,477	0.55	620,220
14	1,760,055	0.82	960,750
15	1,735,382	0.52	579,021

Canadian Table 11: Survey Participants Grouped by 1988 Sales (in Canadian dollars)

Sales	Number of Respondent Companies
Below $250 million	24
$250-500 million	19
$500 million-1 billion	21
$1 billion-2.5 billion	20
$2.5 billion and over	23
Not reporting	4

Canadian Table 12: Survey Participants Grouped by 1988 Assets (in Canadian dollars)

Assets	Number of Respondent Companies
Below $250 million	28
$250-500 million	15
$500 million-1 billion	20
$1 billion-2.5 billion	18
$2.5 billion and over	25
Not reporting	5

Canadian Table 13: Respondents Ranked in *Canadian Business*

Company Rank	Number of Respondent Companies
1-100	32
101-200	24
201-300	16
301-400	13
401-500	11
Other*	15

*Includes banks and insurance companies.

Canadian Table 14: Respondent Companies by Industrial Classification

	Number of Companies
Chemicals	6
Electric machinery & equipment	3
Fabricated metals	2
Food, beverages, tobacco	8
Machinery	5
Paper	9
Petroleum and gas	7
Primary metals	9
Printing and publishing	2
Stone, clay and glass	2
Textiles	2
Transportation equipment	4
Total, Manufacturing	59
Banking	2
Business services	4
Insurance	7
Retail and wholesale trade	11
Telecommunications	10
Transportation	4
Utilities	7
Holding companies	7
Total, Non-Manufacturing	52
Total, All Companies	111

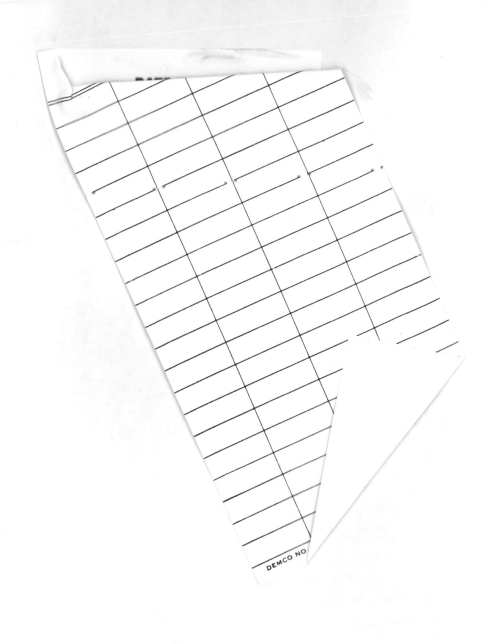

DEMCO NO.